THE SCOUTING GUIDE TO SURVIVAL

THE SCOUTING GUIDE TO SURVIVAL

MORE THAN 200 ESSENTIAL SKILLS FOR STAYING WARM, BUILDING A SHELTER, AND SIGNALING FOR HELP

J. WAYNE FEARS

Skyhorse Publishing

The Boy Scouts of America

Skyhorse Publishing books may be purchased in bulk at
special discounts for sales promotion, corporate gifts,
fund-raising, or educational purposes. Special editions
can also be created to specifications. For details,
contact the Special Sales Department, Skyhorse
Publishing, 307 West 36th Street, 11th Floor, New York,
NY 10018 or info@skyhorsepublishing.com.

Skyhorse® and Skyhorse Publishing® are registered
trademarks of Skyhorse Publishing, Inc.®, a Delaware
corporation.

Visit our website at www.skyhorsepublishing.com.

10 9 8 7 6 5 4 3

Library of Congress Cataloging-in-Publication Data is
available on file.

Cover design by Brian Petersen

Print ISBN: 978-1-5107-3774-7
Ebook ISBN: 978-1-5107-3777-8

Printed in China.

CONTENTS

INTRODUCTION

Each year hundreds of American outdoor enthusiasts find themselves in an unexpected outdoor emergency. They get lost, injured, or stranded and suddenly find themselves cut off from the rest of the world. They suddenly have to depend upon their survival skills to survive. For most people, thanks to modern communications such as cell phones, satellite messengers, and personal locator beacons (PLB), it is merely a sobering two- or three-hour adventure. In fact, with today's high-tech methods of search and rescue, the majority of missing people are found within twenty-four hours, some a sobering seventy-two hours, after they have been reported missing. However, for some who did not take the proper precautions before they left home or do not have survival skills, it can end in tragedy.

Anyone who travels into the backcountry areas near home or deep into the wilderness needs a good working knowledge of basic survival skills. Also, those who travel through, or fly over, unpopulated areas need survival skills. The same can be said for those who venture out onto large bodies of water. Chances are good they will never become stranded in these situations, but if it happens to you, then it is a 100 percent chance.

One of the first questions I hear when conducting survival seminars is this: "Why should anyone learn survival skills?" Then they challenge: "This is the twenty-first century. Wilderness survival is no longer needed."

Few people go into a state park, national forest, or even the woods behind their home expecting to need survival skills. That "it-will-never-happen-to-me" attitude gets untold numbers of people into serious trouble each year. All too often they are found dead near snowbound automobiles, in desert sands, on mountain slopes, near downed aircraft, and in the woods near their homes. They succumb to hypothermia, are struck by lightning, or drown in flash floods. Many panic and start running, often over cliffs. Sometimes they simply lie down and die because of overwhelming fear and the lack of the will to live.

A canoe overturn in swift water can leave the occupants in a survival situation quickly.

A vast majority of people in our technological society think they will never find themselves suddenly cut off from the rest of the world. But the news media often carry stories about people who suffer and die because they don't have even the basic survival skills to keep themselves alive in an emergency. The truth is, a survival crisis can confront anyone suddenly, without warning.

I have spent most of my life in the outdoors studying the challenges of survival. Because of the nature of my career, I've seen both sides of the coin. I have been caught in severe survival situations, and have been on many search-and-rescue missions. Much of what I have learned is in this book.

This book takes to heart the Boy Scout motto of *Be Prepared!* In it we approach the subject of survival from a preparedness standpoint, rather than a collection of pioneering skills and neat tricks that you can't remember, or get to work, when you really need them. I advise the reader that spending time and energy building traps and snares are an unreliable way of getting food if you lack trapping savvy and an above-average knowledge of your quarry. You will not find pages

　　　THE SCOUTING GUIDE TO SURVIVAL

This hunter wisely decided to make a comfortable camp and await rescue rather than attempt to walk out.

of flowering wild plants that are edible because they may not grow where you find yourself in an emergency, and if they do it would probably be in the dead of winter when the plant would be impossible to identify or locate.

This book takes a realistic approach to the subject of survival. Throughout, I stress preparing for the unexpected, beginning before you leave home. My aim is to prepare you, both physically and mentally, to survive those critical first seventy-two hours. The keys are to learn that an emergency can befall you and then know what to do. I hope you will encourage other members of your troop, Explorer Post, family, and friends to learn these skills as well.

The survival training I received from both the Army and the Air Force emphasized eight basic points of survival that have helped get me through many survival situations. As a memory jog, the following acrostic, using the word SURVIVAL, helps in recalling these points, several of which appear over and over again in this book.

Size up the situation
Undue haste makes waste
Remember where you are
Vanquish fear and panic
Improvise
Value living
Act like the natives
Learn basic survival skills

SURVIVAL TRAINING PAYS

Several years ago, when I was working as a wildlife manager in Georgia, I helped lead a search for a missing hunter in the rugged mountains along the Georgia-North Carolina boundary. We were told that this hunter had little hunting experience but had received extensive survival training. In a blinding rainstorm, it took us two days to find the lost hunter. Much to our surprise, when we found him he had almost established a comfortable homestead.

When he first realized he was lost, he stopped walking and picked an opening in the dense woods to establish a survival camp. He immediately put out ground-to-air signals. Realizing bad weather was on the way, he built a shelter under some overhanging rocks that kept him dry and out of the wind. He gathered plenty of firewood and stored it in his shelter. Next, he built a fire, complete with a green log reflector, to keep his shelter warm. It was his fire that led to his being found. The hunter's survival camp was so comfortable that those of us in the search team used it for an overnight rest before packing out the next morning.

Due to his survival training, he lived comfortably through a two-day storm. He stayed positive and worked toward being found. He used the resources at hand to make a survival camp. Will you be like this hunter if your time to spend an unplanned night or two in the woods comes?

HOW TO USE THIS BOOK

1. When you first get this book, sit down and READ it. Think about what you are reading and how it can apply to you and your outings.
2. Reread the chapter on making your survival kit and make a list of the items you need to purchase to put together your own survival kit.
3. On a weekend when you want to do something that is fun and educational, take your survival kit into the woods and spend the night using the items in the kit. Upon completion of the overnight test, be sure to replace any items that may be difficult to repack into a compact package. This exercise may suggest items you will want in your survival kit that my list did not include. Remember it is YOUR survival kit, so modify it to meet your needs.
4. This book does not go into navigational skills. I feel this requires training that, like first aid, you should have before you start going into the backcountry. If you haven't had training in the proper use of your GPS and map and compass, get it ASAP. Learn to use both to travel cross country. It can keep you from ever needing this book.
5. This book does not go into first-aid skills. It is my belief that everyone who ventures into the backcountry should have successfully taken a Red Cross first aid course. Also, those

who have special medical conditions should be skilled in handling them in remote emergencies.

6. Be sure to you always practice the information found in the chapter titled "Before You Go." This will keep your time in a survival situation short.

7. If you find yourself in a lost or stranded situation, stop, sit down, think, remain calm, don't panic, and plan to stay put. By getting control of yourself in these first few minutes, you have increased your survival chances by 50 percent.

8. When you first realize you are in trouble is the time to STOP!

9. As a Maine game warden once said, "Even in today's modern world, there are many trappers and guides who spend the night in the woods with little more than what is found in a basic survival kit. They spend their lives doing it. Relax. You may even enjoy your unplanned stay in the woods."

Finally, the purpose of this book is to help you prepare for that "unplanned night or nights in the woods." With the proper preparation for an outdoor activity, there should be little reason for a survival emergency. But if it should be your time to have to survive several days, this book will have you prepared to do it with style. Survival knowledge and training pays off when the chips are down. Remember, the best survival kit you have is your mind. Feed it survival knowledge, and it will be ready when that knowledge is needed.

Be Prepared!

RESCUE IS USUALLY QUICK

With today's means of communications and transportation, few emergencies go unnoticed for long. Once the word goes out that a person is missing, even in remote areas search crews usually arrive on the scene within a few hours.

SEARCH AND RESCUE SATELLITE AIDED TRACKING

Around the world … around the clock … the National Oceanic and Atmospheric Administration (NOAA) stands watch. As an integral part of worldwide search and rescue, NOAA operates the Search and Rescue Satellite Aided Tracking (SARSAT) system to detect and locate mariners, aviators, and recreational enthusiasts with Personal Locator Beacons (PLB) in distress almost anywhere in the world, at any time, and in almost any condition.

The SARSAT system uses NOAA satellites in low-earth and geostationary orbits as well as GPS satellites in medium-earth orbit to detect and locate aviators, mariners, and land-based users in distress. The satellites relay distress signals from emergency beacons to a network of ground stations and ultimately to the US Mission Control Center (USMCC) in Suitland, Maryland. The USMCC processes the distress signal and alerts the appropriate search-and-rescue authorities to who is in distress and, more important, where they are located. Truly, SARSAT takes the "search" out of search and rescue!

Individual situations such as plane crashes, automobile breakdowns, snakebites, stranded boats, or missing persons are usually brief if the simple precautions given in this book have been taken. If you have taken the time and precaution to file a trip plan with responsible adults before your outing, then you will not go unnoticed for very long if you do not return on time or if you have a medical emergency. This will begin a series of reactions that will result in your being rescued quickly. If this one rule of common sense–to file a trip plan–were followed more often, fewer people would die and most would be rescued in hours rather than days each year.

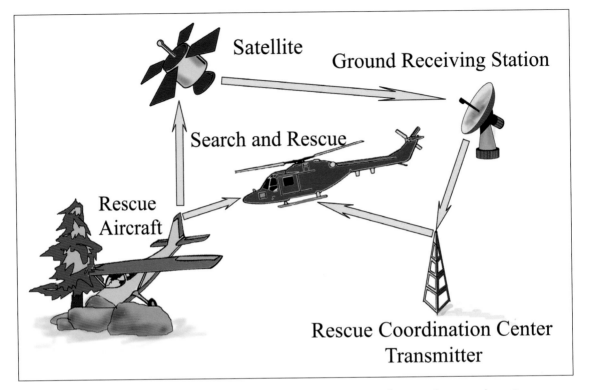

Modern technology uses satellites to locate an emergency beacon's exact location.

One of the most common and dangerous fears most lost or stranded people have is that no one will know to come looking for them. If you have followed the steps in the next chapter of this book, then you can put this fear to rest, as trained people will be looking for you soon. If you stay put once you realize you are lost or stranded, then you will be found in a short period of time. Trying to walk out, panicking, and running will work against you; it will take much longer for rescuers to find you. For every hour a lost person walks, the search area grows four times larger. You should stay put and wait to be found!

HERE IS AN EXAMPLE OF HOW IT WORKS

A search starts quickly when someone is reported missing to local authorities. In most cases this is the county sheriff, district forest ranger, or conservation officer. If it is a boat not returning from an offshore trip on large bodies of water, the Coast Guard will launch a search-and-rescue mission.

Today the National Park Service, many rural fire departments, sheriff departments, and other agencies have experienced search and rescue teams that have received formal training in search and rescue organization and techniques. They know how to respond quickly to a missing person emergency, no matter the terrain or weather. Also available for search and rescue are valuable

Early in the search, specially trained dogs may be used to trail a missing person.

resources such as trained search dogs, fast-water rescue teams, high-angle rescue teams, and helicopters with thermal imaging capability.

When the missing outdoor person report is turned in, the first step usually taken is that a "search boss" is designated. This is someone with experience and training in searches in the backcountry. He sets up the search organization and priorities. He will quickly protect the site where the person was last seen, set up a search headquarters, and interview those people who were last with the missing person, or who know the person well.

Protecting the "last seen" area keeps well-meaning people from destroying tracks and important signs that expert trackers will need for tracking the lost person.

The interview with the missing person's friends/family is most important, as this is where the search boss learns much about the missing person. If a trip plan has been left with someone, it will cut down on the time it takes to get an organized search started. They will have a good idea where to search.

The interviewer will be looking for detailed information on the missing person. This would include the person's name, address, description, clothing worn, boot type (sole information is

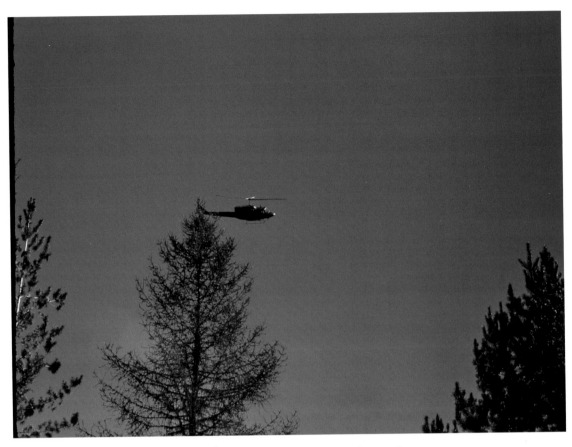

Aircraft are often used to quickly locate lost or stranded people.

important to trackers), age, equipment he has with him, medical condition (including medications), experience in the outdoors, physical condition, personality traits, and so on. All of this information is important to experienced searchers because it tells them a lot about where to look for the missing person.

Usually the first searchers on the search are trackers with dogs and a hasty team. The hasty team is made up of highly specialized people who go into the most likely areas the missing person is believed to be. This is the reason to stay put when you first realize you are lost.

At the same time, lookouts and road-check teams are posted. Lookouts are located at observation points in the search area, and road-search teams ride roads near the search area looking, and listening, for the missing person.

Aircraft, often with specialized equipment, will be brought into the search as quickly as possible. From this point on, the search boss may set up grid searches supervised by professionals, using volunteers.

Many lost people fear that searchers will only look for a few hours and give up, thinking the missing person is dead. This is not true. Most search bosses have a method of estimating how long the missing person can survive under the local conditions and then plan to search three times that long, if needed. Search efforts go far beyond reasonable expectations.

Lost and stranded people should never give up hope, for the search will go on until you are rescued. How fast the search begins depends upon how well you prepared before you went into the woods!

SAR North of the Border

Due to its vast size and range of environments, Canada relies on a diverse group of government, military, volunteer, academic, and industry partners to provide overall search and rescue (SAR) services to the public. SAR is a shared responsibility among federal, provincial/territorial, and municipal organizations, as well as air, ground, and maritime volunteer SAR organizations. There is a distinct organizational difference between the responsibility for ground SAR (GSAR) and that of aeronautical and maritime SAR.

The National Search and Rescue Program (NSP) is a Canada-wide horizontal program that integrates organizations and resources involved in the provision of search and rescue services to Canadians, including SAR response and prevention. The responsibility for the NSP resides within Public Safety and Emergency Preparedness Canada, through the National Search and Rescue Secretariat (NSS). The NSS's role is to serve as a central coordinator for the National SAR Program, working directly with federal, provincial, and territorial organizations, as well as air, ground, and marine volunteer SAR organizations involved in search and rescue activities.

BEFORE YOU GO

A quick rescue actually begins before you get lost or stranded. It begins with you taking some precautions before you leave home, camp, or vehicle. Here are some commonsense precautions for an outing:

KNOW THE AREA IN WHICH YOU PLAN TO TRAVEL

When planning any trip, be sure to take the time to study USGS topographical maps of the area in detail. Pull the area up on Google Earth and see it from above. Studying up on an area in which you plan on exploring is part of the fun of the adventure. It never ceases to amaze me how many people go into the backcountry without knowing the lay of the land, the steepness, where the streams are located, where safe drinking water may be found, the directions roads run, and other essential information. If you get to know the entire area–a much larger area than the specific location you are going–beforehand, you will be able to plan an alternate route in an emergency, if needed.

Studying maps can also alert you to hidden dangers, such as streams that may be prone to flash floods in unusually heavy rainfall, terrain much steeper than you had anticipated, areas subject to avalanche, and so on. Get advice from someone who is reliable and knows the area firsthand. In parks and forests run by government agencies, this information is available from local rangers. Industrial forests, such as those owned by pulp and paper companies and timber companies, have foresters who can help prepare you for their property. The more you know about an area before going into it, the safer your trip will be.

KNOW THE AREA WEATHER EXTREMES

If an area is subject to midsummer snowstorms, hail, lightning, flash floods, or other such real extremes, you should know about them in advance. Be sure to take clothing and equipment needed for protection in the worst weather situation. You never know. You could be caught on the side of a mountain in a sudden snowstorm in July, wearing only hiking shorts and a short-

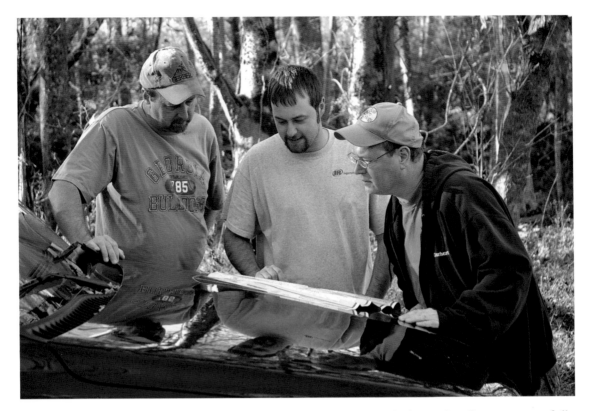

Before venturing into the backcountry, study maps and extended weather forecasts carefully and plan the event to avoid unexpected extremes.

sleeved shirt. Extra clothing could save your life. Always dress for the weather expected and carry clothing for weather extremes in your daypack.

CARRY A FRESHLY CHARGED CELL PHONE THAT HAS A LOCAL WEATHER APP

While there are areas of the country where cell phones lose a signal, these areas become fewer every year, and even when you cannot get a signal strong enough to talk to someone, texting an emergency message is still often possible. Today, the response time to lost or a stranded person has been greatly reduced due to the lost, injured, or stranded person being able to make a cell call to 911 or to a responsible person.

Also, since most areas offer weather apps, it is easy to check the weather as you travel. If you do not have a weather app, a small battery-operated NOAA weather radio can be a lifesaver if a dangerous storm is approaching just over the mountain and out of sight from you. This should never take the place of an advanced careful study of the weather forecast for the area you plan on traveling.

CONSIDER CARRYING A PERSONAL LOCATOR BEACON

For those who want extra protection or for longer trips deeper into the backcountry, consider taking a currently programmed Personal Locator Beacon (PLB). These instruments can feed reports from you, by way of satellite relay, to someone you designate, complete with an accurate location of you on a map. I use a Spot PLB, which gives a critical, life-saving line of communication when you travel beyond the boundaries of cell service. The latest generation of Spot PLBs lets family and friends know you're okay, or, if the worst should happen, sends emergency responders your need for help and GPS location–all with the push of a button. Add this weatherproof, pocket-sized PLB to your essential gear and you can stay connected wherever you roam. Just remember that the service is by subscription, so be sure the PLB you use is current on the subscription plan.

ALWAYS CARRY A SURVIVAL KIT

Equipment for any trip into the backcountry, even a short day hike, should include a survival kit. Later in this book you will find an entire chapter devoted to survival kits. Read it and make a survival kit to keep with your outdoor gear.

UNDERSTAND THE NEED FOR NAVIGATIONAL AIDS

Anyone who plans to go into a backcountry area should have a GPS unit as well as a compass and map of the locale and the skills to use them. Many canoeists and kayakers floating streams and lakes think they don't need navigational aids, but an island-dotted wilderness lake or a difficult cross-country portage can change their minds in a hurry. Anyone going into the wilderness by any means—vehicle, aircraft, skis, snowshoes, horse, whatever—should have and know how to use a GPS unit, a topo map, and a compass. Start the trip by using the navigational aids. Once you realize you are lost is the wrong time to break out the compass.

A PLB, such as the Spot, can keep backcountry travelers in touch with responsible people on a regular basis thanks to the use of satellites.

TAKE OTHER NECESSARY ITEMS

When traveling in, over, or through wilderness country, take other items necessary for your own special needs. If you take medication and are going on a one-day trip, take enough for several days. In a wilderness area, I once had to bring out a diabetic camper who had forgotten his insulin and gone into shock. If you wear glasses or contact lenses, always carry a spare pair and keep them with you. Spare hearing-aid batteries are often overlooked, and if you can't hear searchers it will take much longer to be found

FILE A TRIP PLAN

This is one of the most important survival rules: Before any trip into the backcountry, or anywhere else for that matter, you should file a trip plan with at least two responsible people who will know what to do if you do not return when expected.

The trip plan should include the following information:

1. Your name, address, and cell phone number.
2. Name and phone number of someone in the area of your destination who could be called if you do not return as planned. For instance, if you are hiking in a state park far from where you live, list the state park manager's name and phone number. Having that available can save lots of time getting help on the way to you.
3. Destination name of the location you will be traveling to, or along. Give an exact location, on a topo map if possible. It is difficult to begin a search for someone if their trip plan lists the destination as the Cole National Forest, when Cole National Forest contains forty-five square miles of forestlands. Be specific and mark on the topo map the route you plan to take. If you are on a kayak trip and putting into a river at one point and taking out miles downstream, be sure to indicate these points on the map. If you plan to return to the starting point, also indicate that.
4. Purpose of the trip. Always let someone know the purpose of your trip. Is it for photographing wildflowers, climbing the rock face of a mountain, canoeing, or backpacking? If you do not return, this will give rescue teams valuable information for planning their search, as well as some idea of what could have happened.
5. Mode of transportation. If you plan to drive to a trailhead in your vehicle and then hike from that point into the backcountry, include that in your trip plan. Be sure to indicate where you will leave your vehicle. It is a good idea to record your vehicle license number in your trip plan. That way, if you don't return on time, searchers will know when they have found the right vehicle. This gives them the starting point for their search.
6. Departure date and time.
7. Planned return date and time. Try to be as accurate as possible in estimating your return, and if there is any change in the return date, notify the person who has the trip plan. If notification is impossible, do everything possible to stay with the trip plan. This could prevent an unnecessary full-scale search.
8. Names and addresses of everyone going on the trip. Include the ages of the people on the trip. Many times this information is helpful to search and rescue officials.

If you are departing from a vehicle, be sure to park the vehicle in an area where it can be found easily. Leave a slip of paper in a clear plastic bag with your name, emergency phone number, date/time of departure, description of destination, and expected return date/time. Place this bag under the windshield wiper of the vehicle. This will probably be the starting point of the search when the person you left your trip plan with notifies the authorities that you are missing. Also, this serves as a backup in case something happens to that person you left responsible to monitor your trip plan. This is an extra safety precaution

Taking these precautions is about as important as packing a survival kit. If a responsible person doesn't know you are overdue from your scheduled return, regardless of how short the trip, then no one will know to start looking for you. People have been lost for days before anyone realized there was a problem. In these cases survival ceased to be a short-term emergency and became a long-term nightmare, often with a disastrous ending.

DON'T FAIL TO TAKE THESE PRECAUTIONS!

There are many factors that could prevent your returning as planned, and filing a trip plan could be a lifesaver. Two brothers from Alabama found this out when bad weather put them two weeks behind schedule on a six-hundred-mile kayak trip in the Canadian Arctic.

The pair began their journey after filing a trip plan at Fort Reliance, Northwest Territories. They fell behind schedule when strong winds made the river too rough for paddling and limited their progress to only a few miles a day. To add to their troubles, the kayak was damaged in rapids and they had trouble repairing a hole in it. Then a blizzard struck, and they were forced to stay in their tent three days. By then, the men knew they were in trouble. But fortunately, they had filed a trip plan. When they didn't show up at their destination on time, the Royal Canadian Mounted Police began a search.

Meanwhile, the brothers started rationing their food, which for the last week of their ordeal amounted to a spoonful of lard and a spoonful of oatmeal a day.

Hoping to be spotted by a rescue plane, the men prepared a reflector mirror and kept bright items handy to use to attract attention of search planes. But when the first search plane did fly overhead, a mist obscured them from the plane's view. The plane made a second pass but then flew off as one brother waved an orange gear

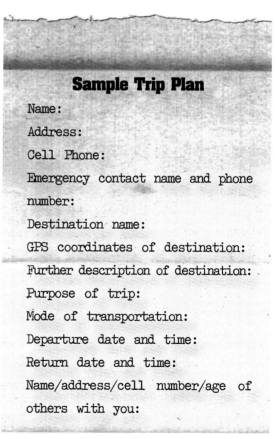

Sample Trip Plan

Name:

Address:

Cell Phone:

Emergency contact name and phone number:

Destination name:

GPS coordinates of destination:

Further description of destination:

Purpose of trip:

Mode of transportation:

Departure date and time:

Return date and time:

Name/address/cell number/age of others with you:

bag. They tried to believe they'd been spotted and that help would arrive, but as the next day dragged by without rescue, they began to have doubts.

Then late that next day, after nine weeks in the Arctic, they heard a helicopter and raced from the tent, desperately waving sleeping bags. This time they were spotted and their long, cold ordeal ended.

As these two men will surely tell you, filing a detailed trip plan could save your life. But always remember to terminate the trip plan as soon as you return. I have been involved in several search and rescue operations in which the person we were looking for turned up safe and sound—down the road at a motel; at a friend's house; or, in the case of one extensive search, at a bar buying drinks for everyone to celebrate a successful whitewater kayak run. It is irresponsible to have a trip plan on file with someone and then fail to notify them when the trip is complete. Search-and-rescue operations are expensive, time-consuming, potentially dangerous to searchers, and emotionally wrenching to family members, who often fear the worst.

3

BE EQUIPPED FOR UNEXPECTED WEATHER

As often as not, bad weather is the cause of people in the outdoors getting lost or stranded. Having a means of keeping up with the weather is important. One of the most valuable tools any outdoorsman can have with him is a small NOAA weather-band radio. They can be purchased at many outdoor stores. The NOAA Weather Radio System broadcasts timely weather information for local areas across the US on a twenty-four-hour basis. The network is capable of reaching 90 percent of all Americans. Canada has a similar system called Weatheradio Canada.

Some weather-band radios are equipped with an alarm feature so that they will come on automatically when severe weather threatens. Most of the weather-band radios operate on a battery, making them convenient to carry into the backcountry.

Another great tool to use in keeping up to date with the local weather is a cell phone with a weather app that gives alerts if bad weather is approaching an area.

Make a cell phone with weather app or weather-band radio a must-have item of equipment for your gear, especially if the outing is a multi-day event. Use it before every outing! Before going into the woods for any period of time, take a few minutes and listen to the weather radio for forecasts of the weather during the period you will be outside. Then dress for the expected weather.

DRESS FOR THE UNEXPECTED

Whether you realize it or not, your clothing is a major part of your survival gear. It is your first line of defense against what nature throws against you. Even in areas of mild weather, the temperature can change dramatically as the time of day changes. Deserts that are hot during the day can be cold at night. Sudden rain showers with wind can change a mild day into a cold day. Climbing steep mountains can cause a person to sweat, getting his clothing wet, which can be cold in the wind.

The point is, always expect the unexpected when planning an outing. Dress to be comfortable, as a specific area dictates, but always be prepared for unexpected weather changes. The best

13

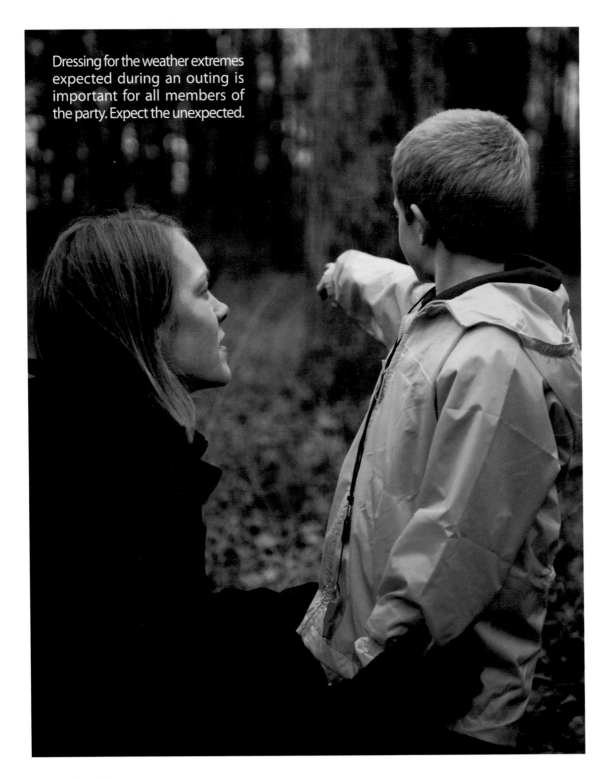

Dressing for the weather extremes expected during an outing is important for all members of the party. Expect the unexpected.

way to do this is to dress in layers: Base layer is underwear, middle layer is the layer that protects the body, and the outer layer is the layer that shields the body from wind, snow, rain, and the elements.

For warm weather the base layer—underwear and T-shirt—can be made of cotton or polyester. Today most experienced hikers choose synthetic fabric such as polyester, as this synthetic material can dry quickly and is lightweight. Cotton is comfortable but when it gets wet it is slow to dry. The middle layer might be a shirt and shorts made of cotton, polyester, or a cotton/nylon blend. Again, cotton can be slow to dry, and if a cool wind is blowing cotton can be cool. In open woodlands the shirt may have short sleeves, but in country with insects, thick brush, or lots of sun exposure, the shirt may have long sleeves to provide more protection, and you may choose to wear lightweight long pants. The head should be covered in a lightweight nylon or polyester broad-brimmed hat. For the outer layer a lightweight polyester fleece jacket may be carried in the daypack along with a lightweight breathable rain suit made from synthetic materials. Boots should be well broken in and be designed to match the weather and terrain.

If the outing is in cool or cold weather, then the layers will start with a base layer of thick polyester underwear capable of wicking moisture away from the body. The middle layer will be long pants and a long-sleeve shirt. The shirt may be made of wool, which will stay warm even when wet, and the pants may be wool blend or polyester fabric depending upon the cold anticipated. A polyester or wool sweater may be worn. Polyester fleece is warm, even when damp, but does not block the wind. The outer layer can be a wool jacket or synthetic insulated jacket. Down insulation is great until it gets wet, then it loses its insulating value. Fleece gloves with weatherproof shell will protect the hands. A fleece or wool stocking hat would be worn. Wool or wool blend socks would be worn inside well-broken-in insulated boots designed for the terrain to be encountered.

It does not take much space in a daypack to include a quality breathable rainsuit. It may come in handy on a dry day as a windbreak and, if it's brightly colored, it can be a good signal. If you get lost or stranded, you may be out a day or two longer than you expected; the weather may change, so outer layer clothing suitable for the weather encountered is good insurance.

Fabrics, insulation, and designs of outdoor clothing are changing rapidly, so it is wise to study what is available on the market today and match it to the conditions you anticipate on your outings. Proper clothing is part of the survival plan.

Dress for the expected weather temperature extremes for the period you are expecting to be out. Dress in layers so that you can remove layers and put in your daypack as the temperature warms up, or as you exert yourself. As the temperature goes lower, or you slow down exertion, you can put the layers back on.

Most important, don't go off without a hat. During cool or cold weather as much as 10 percent of your body heat loss can be from the uncovered head. This can be critical during a period of survival, especially during the night when you are trying to rest.

Wear clothing to match the climate and listen to the weather-band radio or weather app for weather changes. Don't push your luck in bad weather. If bad weather is threatening, cancel your trip—nature will be there another day. A day spent at home during dense fog, snowstorm, thunderstorms, and so on is much better than a night in a survival camp wishing you had canceled the outing.

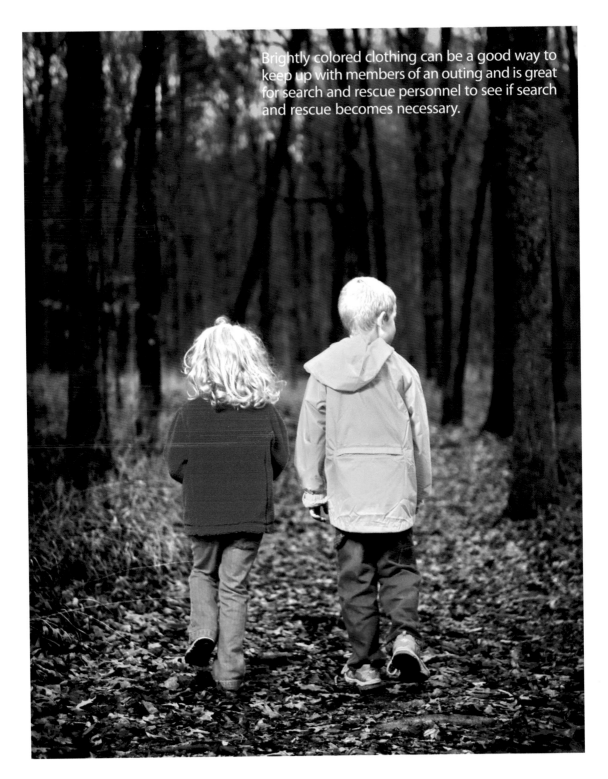

Brightly colored clothing can be a good way to keep up with members of an outing and is great for search and rescue personnel to see if search and rescue becomes necessary.

THE SCOUTING GUIDE TO SURVIVAL

TAKE CARE OF YOURSELF AND YOUR EQUIPMENT

People who have been lost or stranded are frequently in sad physical and mental states when they are found. They are cut, bruised, and dirty. Their clothing is badly torn or lost altogether. Many times they are confused and very frightened.

Just because you are out in the wilderness is no reason to become careless about your body. In fact, the absence of nurses and doctors out there makes it even more important to take care of yourself and try to stay clean. A cut or sore that would be considered trivial in the city could be a life-threatening wound in certain survival situations.

Also, take care of your clothing, because it is a vital part of your survival gear. Your clothes help protect and maintain your body. Try to keep your clothing clean and dry. Clean clothing is warmer. Do not lose your clothing. Make repairs in clothing as needed.

Also, do not do what many lost people do when panic sets in and give in to the urge to run and discard items of clothing as they run. I have seen hikers and hunters who, when they became lost and started to run through the woods, discarded daypacks or hunting vests that contained plenty of items that could have been used to spend an unplanned night in the woods safely. One lost hunter I helped track had discarded his coat, hat, and hunting vest that contained matches, candy, a flashlight, and a small first-aid kit. He was found nearly naked, drowned in a beaver swamp.

4

THIS TWO-POUND SURVIVAL KIT COULD SAVE YOUR LIFE

A survival kit offers excellent insurance for anyone who travels, regardless of whether the mode of transportation is skis, snowshoes, aircraft, boat, canoe, snowmobile, four-wheel-drive vehicle, ATV, automobile, horse or mule, or on foot.

Having a survival kit is only part of the solution, however. One must know how to use the items in the kit in order to survive. I know of an avid canoeist who carried a little survival kit with him on every trip for years. Then he lost his canoe and gear in a set of rapids on a wilderness trip in Minnesota, and he almost died because he panicked and didn't know how to use the contents of his survival kit. Learn how to use the items in your survival kit!

The survival kit is important not only for its life-saving merits, but for comfort on those outings when a night must be spent in the woods or streamside, unexpectedly. I have been forced on

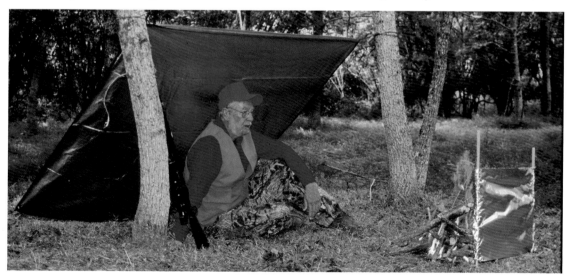

The ingredients found in a simple survival kit make a survival camp such as this possible.

many occasions to spend an unexpected night or two in the woods, nights I didn't plan on, because an outfitter was late picking me up, climbing down a mountain in the dark was too dangerous, a motor conked on my boat, a glacier-melt-swollen creek blocked my return, and so on. Each time, my two-pound survival kit provided me with a comfortable camp. Without it, the waits would have been cold and dangerous.

Regardless of what type of survival kit you decide you need and whether you buy a commercial kit or put together your own, the kit must provide the basic life-saving functions for at least seventy-two hours. If you are short any of the items to meet these needs, then you don't have an adequate survival kit. The items in your kit should enable you to do the following things:

SHELTER

The first item necessary for a survival camp is shelter. You can read all you want about a lean-to, brush shelters, and wickiups, but few shelters are quicker to erect and give as much protection, especially in rain and wind, as a plastic tube tent. You simply tie a length of paracord between two trees, stretch the tube to its full eight-foot length, and crawl in out of the weather. I use the Coghlan's Tube Tent. It is compact, weighs eighteen ounces, and is a bright orange color, serving as a signal as it can be easily seen from the air. Not only have I used a tube tent in a survival situation, I have used one on several occasions for protection from a sudden rain or hail storm when I didn't have a rain suit or other protection. A fifty-foot length of paracord in your survival kit is a great aid to shelter building and many other survival camp chores.

SLEEP WARM

To stay warm in your tube tent, you will want one of the thirty-six-by-eighty-four-inch MCR Medical emergency sleeping bags. This bag, which folds up to one and a half by three inches and weighs only four ounces, will reflect and retain 90 percent of radiated body heat. You will need to be careful using one of these bags, as boots with aggressive soles can cause them to tear. But, with a little caution when getting into the bag, it will keep you warm all night. When on guided trips I carry an extra bag, as I want my guide to be rested in order to get me out safely the next day. Also, an extra bag, while weighing little and taking up little space in my survival kit, gives me a backup if I should tear the first one.

FIRE SOURCE

To build a fire you will need *fresh* strike-anywhere kitchen matches in a waterproof match box (safe). I use the full-size wooden matches because they are easy to ignite and burn longer than small matches. I keep them in a weather-tight bright orange plastic match safe. For backup, a pocket-size butane lighter works well in most situations. If using a pocket-size butane lighter, be sure that it rides in your survival kit where the gas control button is not depressed. I have seen butane lighters removed from a survival kit and the owners were shocked that all the gas had escaped.

I also keep a FireSteel magnesium rod in my kit as a third method of starting a fire. This quality-made magnesium rod can be used to start a fire quickly and easily if you have good tinder. Be cautious when shopping for magnesium rods, as there are a lot of cheap brands on the market

This approximate two-pound survival kit has all the ingredients necessary to sustain life for seventy-two-plus hours.

that do not work well. Practice using the magnesium bar at home before taking it into the wilderness. A survival situation is the wrong time to learn to use this method of starting a fire.

FIRE TINDER

Since starting a fire can be difficult, especially in windy or damp conditions, a package of man-made tinder is a must. While there are several brands of man-made tinder available in outdoor shops and catalogs, I make my own by rubbing petroleum jelly into 100 percent cotton balls and storing them in waterproof medicine bottles. To not carry proven tinder is to ask for trouble when a fire is a must in a driving rainstorm and warmth is critical. This is not to say that you should forget about learning the many forms of tinder that are available naturally, such as birch bark, an old bird's nest, thistle down, sedge grass, and punk, but when a fire is needed fast these natural tinders are often in scarce supply.

SIGNALING

Two methods of signaling should be carried. I suggest a signal mirror, such as a Star Flash floating mirror, and a high-quality whistle, such as a Fox 40 or WindStorm whistle. With practice, the signal mirror is easy to use and can be seen up to sixty miles or more. High-quality whistles require very little energy to use, can be heard much farther than the human voice, and last much longer. Avoid cheap whistles; they are not loud enough and some require a lot of breath to blow.

INSECT CONTROL

For protection against mosquitoes I carry small packets of BugX insect-repellent towelettes. They take up very little space in the survival kit and are worth their weight in gold during warm weather.

LIGHT

I include a small Surefire flashlight in my kit. I like the small flashlights that use LED bulbs and lithium batteries, due to their reported ten-year shelf life. A small LED high-quality flashlight can be used for signaling and is a must for doing camp chores in the dark. Some flashlights come pre-programmed to flash SOS in Morse code. Remember that the flashlight batteries in your survival kit flashlight need to be checked for freshness before you go on any outing.

SAFE WATER

While food need not be a concern for a seventy-two-hour ordeal, water will be necessary. Since safe drinking water has become scarce even in the most remote wilderness areas, it is a good idea to take along either a personal water filter such as Sawyer Mini filter or a small bottle of Potable Aqua tablets to treat drinking water. One of the most versatile items I carry in my survival kit is a twenty-four-inch by twenty-four-inch piece of heavy-duty aluminum foil folded up to about three by three inches. It can be used to make a vessel for boiling water, cooking food, making a reflector for a fire, and as a signal mirror. Pack your survival kit in a one-gallon Ziploc bag and that can be used to hold water while treating.

DUCT TAPE

Duct tape can be used for many purposes in a survival situation. I have used it for patching a hole in my canoe, taping a tear in my emergency sleeping bag, to hold a splint in place, and more. Wrap a three-foot length of duct tape to your flashlight to have on hand when it's needed. I find that wrapping it on my flashlight lets me hold my light in my teeth when I need both hands free at night.

This suggested survival kit is compact, lightweight, and takes up little space in a daypack, hunting coat or fishing vest.

KNIFE

Like most survival instructors, I consider a knife one of the most valuable survival tools to have on hand. Some people like to carry a high-quality folding knife in their survival kit. I like to have a fixed-blade knife on my belt where it is fast and easy to get to in an emergency. I also find that a good fixed-blade knife will handle larger cutting chores better than smaller folding knives will. This is a matter of preference, but a quality knife is a must in a survival situation.

It is not sufficient to purchase all these items and put them in your daypack, tacklebox, or coat pocket to be there when you need them. As with any other specialized outdoor gear, you need to give them a field test, actually use them overnight, so you are familiar with them when you need them. You may find you want to include more items.

Also, if you take medication or wear glasses, you may want to take extras in your kit. A charged cell phone, while not a part of the kit, is also good to carry.

It is a good idea to check your survival kit often to make sure your items are all there and in good shape. Some items, such as matches, must be replaced periodically.

Be sure to keep your survival kit compact and easy to pack or carry. Large survival kits have a way of being left behind. A small, compact kit is easy to carry with you.

Suggested Items for the Personal Survival Kit

- Coghlan's tube tent
- Strike-anywhere kitchen matches in an orange waterproof match safe
- FireSteel magnesium rod
- Butane lighter
- SureFire LED flashlight
- Fire tinder–petroleum jelly cotton balls in waterproof container
- StarFlash floating signal mirror
- Fox 40 or WindStorm whistle
- MRC Medical emergency sleeping bag
- Paracord—fifty feet
- Aluminum foil–36"X36"
- BugX insect-repellent towelettes
- Duct tape–three feet wrapped around flashlight or water bottle
- Potable Aqua water purification tablets or Sawyer mini-filtration device
- Re-sealable heavy-duty plastic bag–one gallon
- Quality pocketknife or belt knife

These items make up your personal survival kit. When combined with your map, compass, GPS, and cell phone, it gives you the edge you need to survive.

SURVIVAL PRIORITIES

Your most important survival skill is your ability to admit that you are lost or stranded. That is not an easy decision to make. Most people will not admit that until they have wandered around for long periods and gotten into a worse situation than they would have been in had they admitted their predicament at the beginning.

Once you admit that you are lost or stranded, sit down and think. If you have a cell phone, now is the time to call for help and await the help. Get control of yourself, avoid panic, and stay calm. Mentally you must accept the challenge you are facing and make the best of the adventure. If you left a trip plan with a responsible person, chances are that people will be looking for you soon. Your adventure will be short lived. Even in remote regions of North America, 99 percent of the missing people on outings are found within seventy-two hours or less. You will be too.

Let's face it, avoiding panic is difficult when dealing with yourself or, if you are not alone, with those people in your group. Most people who get lost or stranded panic to some degree, but those who fare best are those who get control of panic quickly. In extreme cases, those who panic may forget who they are or where they are. Some even hide from searchers. This erratic behavior makes it difficult for searchers to find them. Later in this chapter are the seven survival priorities to prevent panic.

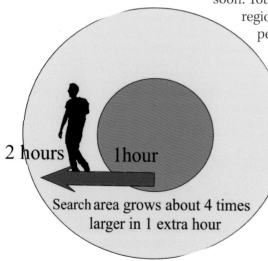

2 hours 1 hour

Search area grows about 4 times larger in 1 extra hour

As this chart shows, the longer a lost person walks the greater the search area becomes, resulting in a long-delayed rescue.

STOP

The first thing to do when you admit to yourself that you are lost or stranded is to resist the temptation to walk or run your way out of the situation. STOP! This is the acronym for:

Sit
Think
Observe
Plan

Follow this simple plan of controlling panic.

Sit: The act of sitting down will help keep you from getting into deeper trouble. This one act alone can also start the thinking process, and it helps suppress the urge to run or to make hasty, foolish decisions. You will need this time to get over the shock that it has happened to you: YOU ARE LOST.

Think: Survival is the challenge to stay alive. Your mind is the best survival kit you have. In a survival situation, you are at the mercy of your mind. In order to survive, you must keep control of your mind by thinking of past training, by maintaining a positive mental attitude, and by determination.

Think about what survival instructors call the Rules of Three:

- You may be doomed in three seconds if you let panic rule.
- You cannot live more than three minutes without oxygen.
- You cannot live more than three hours in temperature extremes without body shelter.
- You cannot live more than three days without water.
- You will begin to need food in three weeks.

These Rules of Three tell you that you need to think of the real and immediate dangers, not those conjured up by your fears. Your most immediate danger is your own mind. Don't let fear take control and cloud clear, resourceful thinking.

Observe: Observe your surroundings to discover what problems must be solved and what resources you have to solve them. You will need shelter, signals, fire, water, and a campsite that is easily spotted. First aid may be needed on yourself or someone else. Select a campsite, get out your survival kit, and set about getting ready to be found. If you are with others, make job assignments. Get everyone involved. Keep all busy. Keep everyone positive.

Plan: Now that you are settled down and ready to live the adventure, make plans to set them in motion. If you are in a group, gather the group and get organized to be found. What do you have that will aid in your survival? What natural materials are at hand? Select a survival campsite. Set out signals. Keep calm and be comfortable out of the weather while you await rescue. Having a plan makes the wait go smoothly and safely.

The STOP acronym has value, so learn it and follow it.

1. Provide First Aid

If you or a member of your group has life-threatening injuries or illness, take action at once to take care of that person. Put your first aid training to work.

2. Seek Shelter

If the weather is extreme or appears to be getting bad, shelter is a top priority. Heat can kill quickly without shade and water. If it is raining and the wind is blowing, hypothermia is a threat that must be taken seriously. Shelter out of the elements is a must.

3. Build a Fire

Fire can be a lifesaver in many ways. It can provide much-needed warmth on cold days, dry wet clothing, be a signal to searchers, boil water for safe drinking, cook food, boost one's spirits, and keep animals at bay. Having fire-making items in your survival kit and knowing how to build a fire are essential survival skills.

4. Signal for Help

Once it is realized that you are in trouble, be it a call on your cell phone or not returning when your trip plan said, a search will be started right away. Having signals out or ready to use at once becomes very important to your being found quickly. Follow the instructions given in this book to make sure your signals can be seen or heard by searchers.

5. Drink Water

Dehydration is a great danger in a survival situation. The body is about 65 percent water and it takes a lot of water, about eight glasses per day, to keep the mind sharp and the body functioning at its peak rate. That is the reason why we suggest that you have methods for making water safe to drink in your survival kit. No outing should be taken without taking plenty of water with you. We devote a chapter of this book on making water found naturally in the wild safe to drink. The body will start shutting down if it is not receiving water within about three days.

6. Don't Worry About Food

Since in all likelihood you will be rescued within seventy-two hours, food is the least likely of your survival priorities. Most of us carry around enough body fat to go many days without eating. Chances are really good that you will be out of the wilderness long before you start losing weight.

7. Have a Will to Live

There have been countless numbers of people who were lost or stranded for weeks without food, fire, or shelter. When they were found, they were in good shape. On the other hand there have been cases where people were lost just a day or so, and they perished. The difference between these people was that those who made it in good condition had a strong WILL TO LIVE. They never gave up hope of being found. They made the best of a bad situation. They didn't panic. They stayed put. They made the best of the resources at hand; and they had, or quickly developed, a positive mental attitude. In today's terms, they kept their cool. You have to value life in order to take charge of your mind and the situation you find yourself in. Give up your value of life and you will not last long.

Once you get over the first shock wave that you are lost or stranded, put a high value on your life and capitalize on your WILL TO LIVE. You will be amazed at what it will get you through.

MANAGING FEAR

Most people think, "Survival training is something I won't need." But each year, thousands of travelers, sportsmen, campers, hikers, and others find themselves suddenly lost or stranded in North America's backcountry, often not too far from home. Here is an example I saw myself several years ago.

It had started out as a typical afternoon squirrel hunt. Three of us had taken an afternoon off to hunt in the big hardwoods found in a nearby national forest. As dusk gave way to darkness, two of us leaned on the car reliving, blow by blow, the accounts of the afternoon hunt. Suddenly it occurred to us that the third member of our party hadn't returned to the car, and darkness had now set in. Yet we didn't worry, since Mike was a trained and experienced outdoorsman. He was working on his master's degree in forest management and had just recently returned from four years of working in the Alaskan backcountry.

After thirty more minutes of waiting, I blew the car horn three times. No response. For the next ten minutes we blew the horn and shouted, stopping occasionally to listen. It was becoming very clear that Mike was in trouble. We began to wonder if he was hurt. Mike was a very safe hunter and was in excellent physical condition, so any questions along those lines seemed to be out of place. The reality that Mike was lost began to sink in. Shortly thereafter, an organized search began.

An hour after midnight, a wild-looking man broke through a thicket and ran into the light cast by the searchers' spotlights. Mike was wide-eyed and confused. His clothing from the waist down was torn to shreds and his legs and arms were bloody from the mass of scratches he had received. The .22 rifle, hunting coat, and cap he had taken into the woods with him were gone, where he did not know. We later learned that his coat contained matches, extra ammunition, a pocketknife, and three squirrels, enough survival items to live comfortably for many days.

It took Mike two weeks to fully recover from his brief but brutal ordeal. He recalled the panic that struck him at dark when he realized he was lost. He remembered running for long periods

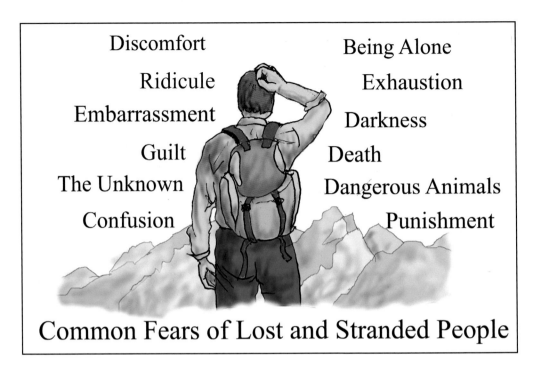

Discomfort

Being Alone

Ridicule

Exhaustion

Embarrassment

Darkness

Guilt

Death

The Unknown

Dangerous Animals

Confusion

Punishment

Common Fears of Lost and Stranded People

of time. He also remembered a feeling of fear toward the strange people shouting and flashing lights in the woods. The feelings of embarrassment, guilt, confusion, and exhaustion all raced through his mind at the same time. Mike, an above-average outdoorsman, had come face to face with a survival situation and had not used the skills to live.

One of the first reactions to being lost or stranded in the backcountry is fear. It is fear that causes many people to panic soon after they realize that they are in a survival situation. It was fear that made Mike run blindly in the dark and discard his equipment.

CAUSES OF FEAR

Here is what research has shown that most people fear in a survival situation:

1. Ridicule or embarrassment: Those I have interviewed soon after rescue said this was the first fear they experienced. This is especially a major fear of experienced outdoorsmen who want to maintain their "Daniel Boone" image.
2. Punishment: It is this fear that causes many lost children and senior citizens to hide soon after they realize they are lost. Coupled with this fear is the fear of being late. Most of us live as slaves to a clock, and when we aren't where we are supposed to be, when we are supposed to be there, we face some form of punishment. This fear of punishment is present in every survival situation.
3. Being alone: Many people have never been truly alone. To them this is a strange and suddenly frightening experience. I once led a small search team for an experienced worldwide

hunter. While he was only lost for a few hours, this man was in shock, as he had never been alone except in a room or other such circumstance. In his travels all over the world, he was always with a guide or group. The few hours he spent lost, alone, caused him to end his hunting career.

4. Animals: Many people have hidden fears of wild animals and sounds in the woods. In my military career, I saw some of the best trained fighters in the world who were frightened of wild animals to the point of becoming less proficient than they could have been. The fear of wild animals is mentioned by many formerly lost and stranded people, especially children. Most people forget under the stress of survival that wild animals prefer to avoid people and, with the exception of an occasional bear or mountain lion, wild animals of North America don't attack people.

5. Darkness: Darkness brings on fear to many people under survival stress. I was once stranded in a remote wilderness with a geologist who was dreadfully afraid of the dark. Each night when it got dark, he would go into a deep sleep and stay in this state of sleep until daylight. Nothing could wake him. In the dark there are sounds which sound menacing and awful and bring on fear. I have heard a beetle crawling in dry leaves sound like an animal weighing one hundred pounds crawling. The night brings out the worst in our imaginations and scares some people to the extreme.

6. The unknown: Coupled with the fear of darkness is the fear of the unknown. Questions like "What should I do? Will anyone look for me? What's that strange noise?" fill the mind of a person under survival stress. Research also shows that people tend to magnify the unknown. The less the mind has to occupy it, the more it will be plagued with the fear of the unknown.

7. Death: Death is something very few people think of or face very often. However, in a survival situation, death is suddenly on the mind. Once in an extreme survival situation in Canada, I saw a man cry and repeat over and over, "I will never see my wife and children again." With this kind of thinking, the will to live cannot enter the mind and death can come about. The fear of death can paralyze one who is not even in a life-threatening situation.

8. Discomfort: This is one of the most common fears. Survival means little rest, sleeping on the ground, drinking muddy water, insect bites, cold, heat, and many other uncomfortable things. While usually not serious, many people in our modern world cannot cope with these possible discomforts and instead panic. Many times, with a little calm thinking, most of these discomforts could be avoided.

9. Ignorance: With proper training, this is one of the fears that could be avoided. This fear is the one that causes the lost person to say, "I don't know the first thing to do. I'm in big trouble!" His first reaction is to run away from the problem. This gets him into more trouble.

Fear may vary widely in intensity, duration, and frequency of occurrence, with effects on behavior ranging from mild discomfort to complete disorganization and panic. Fear may control your behavior, and you may react to your feelings and imagination rather than to the problem that caused the fear. The situations you face in survival are, however, within reasonable bounds.

SIGNS OF FEAR

The physical symptoms of fear include:

- Quickening of pulse, trembling;
- Dilation of pupils;
- Increased muscular tension and fatigue;
- Perspiration of palms of hands, soles of feet, and armpits;
- Dryness of mouth and throat, higher pitch of voice, stammering;
- Feeling of "butterflies in stomach" and emptiness of stomach, faintness, and nausea.

Accompanying these physical symptoms, the following psychological symptoms are common:

- Irritability, increased hostility;
- Talkativeness in early stages, leading finally to speechlessness;
- Confusion, forgetfulness, and inability to concentrate;
- Feelings of unreality, flight, panic, or stupor.

SUGGESTIONS FOR CONTROLLING FEAR

Many of us have come to consider comfort as our greatest need. Comfort is not essential, and we often value it much too highly when the alternative is survival. You must value your life more than your comfort and be willing to tolerate heat, hunger, dirt, itching, pain, and almost any discomfort. If you expose yourself to a bitter cold wind because you have swollen ankles and think you can't walk to the shelter of nearby timber, you have your priorities out of order. The key to this change of attitude is the reason that identifies the pain of walking as a temporary problem compared to freezing to death.

Knowing how much you can take and understanding your demands for comfort will help you endure discomforts, particularly when the discomforts are temporary. Recognition of them as discomforts will help you concentrate on effective action.

Some Suggestions to Help You Control Your Fears

- Survival training, including knowledge and experience gained in simulated situations, has the power to reduce the unknown and contribute to the control of fear.
- Don't run away from fear; recognize it, understand it, admit it, and accept it. Learn what your reactions are likely to be.
- Learn how to think, plan, and act logically even when you are afraid. Doing these effectively is to take positive action to control fear.
- Develop confidence in yourself. Increase your capabilities by keeping physically and mentally fit. Know your equipment and how to use it. Learn as much as you can about all aspects of survival and how much stress you can stand. You will find that you can stand much more than you previously thought you could.

- Be prepared. Accept the possibility that "it can happen to me." Be properly equipped and clothed at all times. Have a plan ready that you have studied. Hope for the best, but be prepared to cope with the worst.
- Keep informed. Read books on survival, such as this one. Know when danger threatens and be prepared if it comes. Increase your knowledge and thus reduce the unknown.
- Keep busy at all times. Do all you can to prevent hunger, thirst, fatigue, idleness, and ignorance about the situation, since these increase fear.
- Know how other members of your group react to stress. Learn to work together in emergencies to live, work, plan, and help each other as a team.
- Practice your religion. If you have spiritual faith, it can be a big help.
- Cultivate good survival attitudes. Keep your mind on your main goal and keep everything else in perspective. Learn to tolerate discomfort. Don't exert yourself to satisfy minor desires which may conflict with your overall goal–to survive.

Controlling Fear in Others

Survival situations such as group outings, natural disasters, stranding, downed aircraft, and stranded vehicles sometimes involve one or more people besides you. They could be family members, fellow Scouts, close friends, or just acquaintances who joined the group for a trip or a hike. In one way, having someone else along makes an emergency situation much easier–it lessens or eliminates the fear of being completely alone. And you have someone to talk to about emergency plans and to help with survival chores.

But there are problems with group survival situations as well. If family members are involved, you may feel responsible for getting loved ones into trouble. Or with acquaintances, you may not know what they can tolerate or how well they will handle fear. While you may be able to keep your own fears in check, someone else may not. That person could easily spread a sense of panic among the others and get everyone into still deeper trouble.

The following are some steps to take when in a group survival situation:

- Cultivate mutual support. The greatest support under severe stress may come from a tightly knit group. Teamwork reduces fear while making the efforts of everyone more effective.
- Use leadership skills. The most important test of leadership, and perhaps its greatest value, lies in the stress situation. Lead by example and encourage others to stay involved.
- Practice discipline. A disciplined group has a better chance of survival than an undisciplined group.
- Use contagion to your advantage. Calm behavior and demonstration of control are contagious. Both reduce fear and inspire courage.

Fear can kill or it can save lives. It is a normal reaction to danger. By understanding and controlling fear through training, through knowledge, through reducing the unknown, and by effective group action, fear can be overcome.

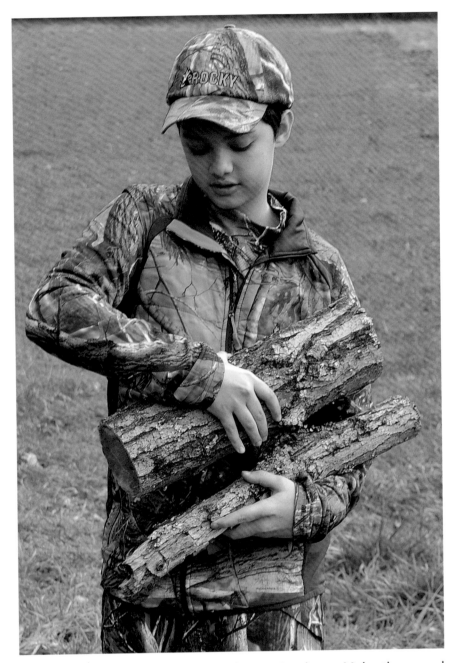

Keep everyone in a group survival situation busy. Make them and their efforts important. Idle time allows the mind to garner fears.

SURVIVAL FIRST AID

One of the major reasons many people get into wilderness survival situations is that they don't take care of themselves. They overexert themselves, they take chances, and they are exposed to weather and other conditions that they aren't accustomed to.

Survival begins at home. No one should venture deep into the backcountry if he or she is not in good health and in a reasonably good state of physical conditioning. Your general state of mental and physical health could determine your ability to survive. A well-nourished person in good physical and mental condition can tolerate a lot of stress and deprivation before becoming incapacitated.

This chapter is not intended to make you a wilderness doctor, nor is it designed to take the place of books that cover the details of emergency first aid. Instead, this chapter will introduce the situations related to your well-being that may develop during a survival ordeal and then explore the means of preventing and handling such situations. In a survival situation you could be days away from medical help, so you must make every effort to avoid illness or injury.

I further recommend that anyone going on a wilderness outing take the Red Cross first aid course and keep the training current. If you are a group leader or if you are planning an extensive backcountry adventure, you should take enough training to become a certified emergency medical technician, or EMT.

MENTAL FIRST AID

In many of the rescue operations I have participated in, the victims were suffering from significant amounts of psychological duress, negative outlooks, even mental breakdowns. These instances reaffirmed for me that survival can greatly depend on one's state of mind.

I have seen some survivors who had no technical survival knowledge or skills but came through their ordeal with flying colors. Why? Because they had a strong positive mental attitude that largely of itself pulled them through. In fact, I think that wilderness survival is almost entirely a mental challenge. It's extremely important to gain control of your mind at the onset of a survival situation and maintain a positive mental attitude throughout the ordeal. Remember that if you take care of your mind first, then your mind will take care of you

If you are in a group survival situation, chances are good that at least one of you is going to be negative-minded. Stress brings out the worst in many people. In this case, you must help the negative-minded person to become positive. Constructive activity, such as shelter improvement and firewood gathering, can help, but your encouragement and positive attitude will do even more.

Make everyone in the survival group a vital and important part of the total effort. This feeling of importance and comradeship can go a long way toward keeping a weaker individual from wallowing in negative thoughts.

FIRST AID KITS

Years ago wilderness travelers had to assemble their own first aid kit or use one of the home varieties. Now there are kits designed specifically for short or long-term wilderness trips. There are kits for the pocket, backpack, boat or canoe, vehicle, remote expeditions, or base camps. I use the Mountain Series Explorer model by Adventure Medical Kits, which is rated for four people for seven days.

This medical kit is equipped for serious first aid for four people for seven days.

Get a first aid kit that best matches the type of trip and length you are planning. If the kit is to serve a group, match the kit to the size of the group. Be sure your kit includes a tube of antiseptic, After Burn, After Bite, and tick removal forceps.

Simply having a first aid kit is not enough in a survival situation. Once you have a kit, study and know when and how to use what is in it. Have the skills to use the first aid supplies when they are needed.

HEAT ILLNESS

Heat is a commonly overlooked danger in the summer backcountry. Let's say the temperature is high and there is little or no breeze. Chances are you're not accustomed to such heat or to the hard work of pulling a loaded canoe over logs, winching a vehicle out of mud, or climbing a steep hill. These conditions can bring on the deadly condition known as "heatstroke" or the less serious condition known as "heat exhaustion." A person does not have to be in the sun to get either of these conditions. A hot, shaded swamp or creek can be enough.

Heatstroke

Energy production in the human body is accompanied by the production of excess heat. To eliminate this heat, the body increases the flow of blood through the skin and stimulates the production of sweat, the body's air conditioner. Through evaporation, convection, and radiation, the body gets rid of excess heat. If a malfunction occurs in the heat-regulating mechanism, the body temperature can zoom to 106°F. Then the body's vital organs—brain, heart, and kidneys—literally cook in their own juices. The result is death. An average of four thousand deaths a year in the US are attributed to heatstroke.

While heatstroke can come on with little warning, its symptoms include the following:

- headache
- dizziness
- lack of sweating
- dry, hot, red skin
- fast, strong pulse
- dilated pupils
- unconsciousness
- temperature over 101°F

Treatment for heatstroke is as follows:

- Move the victim to a cool place and lay him down with his head raised.
- Open the clothing and cool the body down quickly, using every means possible.
- Give slightly salted water, one teaspoon of salt to one quart of water.
- Do not give him drinks that contain caffeine or alcohol.
- Get the victim to a doctor as soon as possible.

Heat Exhaustion

While less serious than heatstroke, heat exhaustion is nothing to ignore. If not treated, heat exhaustion will most likely develop into heatstroke.

The symptoms of heat exhaustion include:

- weakness
- muscle cramps
- headaches
- profuse sweating
- pale, cool, clammy skin (as opposed to hot, dry, and red skin with heatstroke)
- nausea
- normal temperature

Treatment for heat exhaustion is as follows:

1. Move the victim to a cool place and lay him down with his feet slightly raised.
2. Give him slightly salted water to drink.
3. Pour cool water over victim.
4. If recovery is not quick, promptly transport the victim to a doctor.

The best way to cope with the dangers of heatstroke and heat exhaustion is to prevent them. Here are the rules you should follow to prevent heat disorders:

1. Before you go on an outing during the summer, spend two weeks getting acclimated to high temperatures and heavy exertion. For an hour each day, exercise in the heat. Start out slowly and rest often. Remember, heavy exertion in hot climates uses up a lot of the body's liquids. Drink large quantities of Gatorade or bouillon, which are relatively balanced salt solutions.
2. Avoid drugs that promote heatstroke or reduce your natural thirst. Check with your doctor if you are taking sedatives, diuretics, tranquilizers, and such. If you're running a fever, stay home.
3. Wear lightweight, loose-fitting clothing that is white or light tan to reflect the sun's rays. Wear a hat, but make sure it is ventilated to promote evaporative cooling from sweat-soaked hair. Be careful when wearing rain gear because it tends to trap body heat.
4. Stop frequently to cool off. Try wetting your hair.
5. Save heavy chores for early morning and late afternoon, when the air is cooler. Relax during the heat of the day.
Make sure your liquid intake replaces your sweat output. The body requires two quarts of water per day–one quart to moisten lung air, one pint for urine, and one pint for perspiration. Dehydration is an important factor in causing heat disorders.

Signs And Symptoms Of Dehydration At Various Stages Of Body Water Deficiency		
1 to 5 percent *of body weight*	**6 to 10 percent** *of body weight*	**11 to 20 percent** *of body weight*
Thirst	Dizziness	Delirium
Vague discomfort	Headache	Spasticity
Economy of movement	Labored breathing	Swollen tongue
No appetite	Tingling in limbs	Inability to swallow
Flushed skin	Decreased blood volume	Deafness
Impatience	Increased blood concentration	Dim vision
Sleepiness	Absence of salivation	Shriveled skin
Increased pulse	Blue colored body	Painful urination
Increased rectal temperature	Indistinct speech	Numb skin
Nausea	Inability to walk	

DEHYDRATION

Dehydration is caused by failure to correct the body's "imbalance of liquids" by replacing liquid and salt which have been lost, and also by the failure to allow oneself sufficient rest after being engaged in strenuous activities.

The symptoms of dehydration parallel the symptoms of heatstroke and heat exhaustion. The mouth, tongue, and throat become parched and dry, and swallowing becomes difficult. General nausea may be accompanied by spells of faintness, extreme dizziness, and vomiting. A feeling of tiredness and weakness sets in, accompanied by body aches, especially in the legs. In addition, the victim may find it difficult to keep his eyes in focus, and fainting or "blacking out" may occur.

Dehydration incapacitates you for a period of from a few hours to several days. It can be prevented during cold weather by following the same general preventive measures applicable to hot, dry areas. Drink lots of water and/or Gatorade to offset excessive body water losses. The amount will vary according to the individual and the type of exertion. Rest is equally important as a preventive measure. Remember that any work you must do while bundled in several layers of clothing is especially exhausting. This is particularly true of any travel by foot, regardless of how short the distance.

A person who has become dehydrated should be kept warm, but his clothes should be loosened sufficiently to allow proper circulation. Liquids and salt should be fed to him gradually, and, most important of all, he must have plenty of rest.

WINDCHILL																							
WIND SPEED		**TEMPERATURE (°F)**																					
CALM	CALM	40	35	30	25	20	15	10	5	0	−5	−10	−15	−20	−25	−30	−35	−40	−45	−50	−55	−60
KNOTS	MPH	**EQUIVALENT CHILL TEMPERATURE**																				
3–6	5	35	30	25	20	15	10	5	0	−5	−10	−15	−20	−25	−30	−35	−40	−45	−50	−55	−65	−70
7–10	10	30	20	15	10	5	0	−10	−15	−20	−25	−35	−40	−45	−50	−60	−65	−70	−75	−80	−90	−95
11–15	15	25	15	10	0	−5	−10	−20	−25	−30	−40	−45	−50	−60	−65	−70	−80	−85	−90	−100	−105	−110
16–19	20	20	10	5	0	−10	−15	−25	−30	−35	−45	−50	−60	−65	−75	−80	−85	−95	−100	−110	−115	−120
20–23	25	15	10	0	−5	−15	−20	−30	−35	−45	−50	−60	−65	−75	−80	−90	−95	−105	−110	−120	−125	−135
24–28	30	10	5	0	−10	−20	−25	−30	−40	−50	−55	−65	−70	−80	−85	−95	−100	−110	−115	−125	−130	−140
29–32	35	10	5	−5	−10	−20	−30	−35	−40	−50	−60	−65	−75	−80	−90	−100	−105	−115	−120	−130	−135	−145
33–36	40	10	0	−5	−15	−20	−30	−35	−45	−55	−60	−70	−75	−85	−95	−100	−110	−115	−125	−130	−140	−150
WINDS ABOVE 40 MPH HAVE LITTLE ADDITIONAL EFFECT.		LITTLE DANGER					INCREASING DANGER (Flesh may freeze within 1 minute)						GREAT DANGER (Flesh may freeze within 30 seconds)										
		DANGER OF FREEZING EXPOSED FLESH FOR PROPERLY CLOTHED PERSONS																					

Windchill can be increased by activities which take you out into the open where the wind can rob you of body heat. Activities that involve motion can greatly increase the windchill effect.

HYPOTHERMIA

Hypothermia is the major killer of people lost or stranded in the backcountry. Many of those found alive are also suffering from hypothermia, which is a drop in deep body temperature that can be deadly if not detected promptly and treated properly

Hypothermia can strike in any season and in almost any climate. All that is needed is a mild air temperature–30 to 50°F, wetness, rain, sweat, a creek dunking, a slight wind, and a tired person.

Hypothermia attacks a person in two steps. The first is when your body begins to lose heat faster than it produces it. At this point you are aware of feeling cold, and the shivering begins. Usually uncontrollable shivering is the first sign of hypothermia.

The second step is when the cold reaches the brain and deprives you of the ability to make good judgments. Confusion will take over decision making, which is the reason why almost no one recognizes that he or she has hypothermia. In the second step, your internal temperature is sliding downward. Without treatment, this slide leads to stupor, collapse, and death. Each year many people become lost due to confusion brought on by early stages of hypothermia.

There are several ways to avoid hypothermia.

1. Stay dry. When clothing gets wet, it may lose 90 percent of its insulating value. Even sweating can bring on hypothermia.
2. Beware of the wind chill. A slight breeze carries heat away from bare skin faster than still air. It turns wet clothing into a refrigerator due to evaporation.

3. Understand cold. Most hypothermia cases develop in air temperatures that are considered mild, with wind chill temperatures in the 40s and 50s. Most people do not believe such temperatures can be dangerous.
4. Terminate exposure. When you cannot stay warm and dry in existing weather conditions, either get a fire going at a natural shelter out of the wind or set up your tube tent and get into the emergency bag. Get out of the wind and dampness, and get warm, as fast as possible.
5. Never ignore shivering. Persistent or violent shivering is clear warning that you are in the early stages of hypothermia.

When hypothermia symptoms are noticed, treatment should begin immediately.

- First get the victim out of the weather and remove his wet clothing.
- If the victim is only mildly impaired, give him warm drinks and get him into dry clothing and a tube tent and emergency bag.
- If the victim is semi-conscious or worse, he does not have the capability of regaining his body temperature without outside help.
- Keep him awake, give him warm drinks, and if possible get him into a warm bath.
- If possible, strip the victim and put him into an emergency bag with another person. Skin to skin contact is an effective treatment.

As the body core temperature drops, here is how hypothermia affects you:

98.6° to 96°	Uncontrolled shivering, ability to perform complex tasks impaired.
95° to 91°	Violent shivering, difficulty in speaking.
90° to 86°	Shivering decreases, muscles begin to stiffen, coordination is lost. The mind becomes dull; in some cases, amnesia occurs.
85° to 81°	Victim becomes irrational, drifts into stupor. Pulse and respiration are slowed. Muscular rigidity continues.
80° to 78°	Unconsciousness. Reflexes cease to function and heartbeat becomes erratic.
Below 78°	Total failure of cardiac and respiration systems. Death occurs.

Huddle together with sides touching.

Multiple people in cold water can huddle to conserve warmth.

Heat escape lessening posture (HELP)

The HELP position is good for conserving body temperature when immersed in cold water.

In a survival situation, every effort should be made to avoid hypothermia. That means get a warm camp set up before you get wet and cold. Don't put off getting a survival camp established. Delay can be deadly. Avoid hypothermia at all costs!

Cold Water Hypothermia

Survival in cool to cold water depends on many factors. The temperature of the water is only one of them. Others include body size, fat, and activity in the water, to name a few. Large people cool slower than small people. People who are overweight cool slower than thin people. Children, because they are small, cool faster than adults. Anyone swimming or treading water cools faster than those who remain still. An "average" person, wearing light clothing and a personal flotation device (PFD), may survive two and a half to three hours in 50°F water by remaining still. Swimming and treading water increase the cooling rate by about 35 percent.

Many people who find themselves in cold water immediately swim for the shore. If the shore is very near and you are absolutely certain you can make it, then do it, swim for shore. If you do swim, use a flotation device and be sure you have your survival kit.

The Coast Guard advises that if you are hanging on to a floating boat or canoe, you should get as much of your body out of the water as possible. Try to climb back into the boat or canoe or cling to a tree or buoy.

If you are caught out in open water alone, go into what is known as the HELP position (Heat Escape Lessening Posture) to slow down hypothermia. The inner sides of the arms are held tightly against the sides of the chest over the "hot" region and the thighs are raised to protect the groin region. This behavior, effective only when wearing a life jacket, results in nearly a 50 percent increase in predicted survival time.

If you are with a group, huddle. Longer survival time is accomplished when several persons huddle together. Studies show that if a huddle is formed so that the sides of the chests of different persons are held close together, a 50 percent increase in predicted survival time is obtained.

FROSTBITE

Frostbite is the freezing of some part of the body. It is a constant hazard in subfreezing weather, especially when the wind is strong. As a rule, the first sensation of frostbite is numbness rather than pain. You can see the effect of frostbite as a grayish or yellow-white spot on the skin before you can feel it. Therefore, use the buddy system. Watch your buddy's face to see if any frozen spots show; have him or her watch yours.

If frostbite occurs, here are some points to remember:

- Get the person to a heated shelter if possible and remove any wet clothing.
- Unless absolutely necessary, the person should not walk on frostbitten toes or feet.
- Do not rewarm the skin until you can keep it warm. Warming and then re-exposing the frostbitten area to cold air can cause worse damage.
- Gently warm the area in warm water (approximately 110°F) or with wet heat until the skin appears red and warm.

The hand on the right shows the damage caused by frostbite.

- If no water is nearby, breathe on the area through cupped hands and hold it next to your body to aid in thawing.
- Do not use direct heat from heating pads, radiator, or fires.
- Do not rub or massage the skin or break blisters
- Loosely apply dry, sterile dressings.
- Put gauze or clean cotton balls between fingers or toes to keep them separated.

VENOMOUS SPIDER BITE

Unless you actually see and identify the spider that has bitten you, it is very difficult to know what has bitten you.

The black widow spider produces protein venom that affects the victim's nervous system. This neurotoxic protein is one of the most potent venoms secreted by an animal. Some people are slightly affected by the venom, but others may have a severe response. The first symptom is acute pain at the site of the bite, although there may only be a minimal local reaction. Symptoms usually start within twenty minutes to one hour after the bite.

Another toxic spider is the brown recluse, whose venom is more potent than that of a rattlesnake and is toxic to cells and tissues. However, because the bite releases much smaller quantities of poison into its victims, brown recluse bites cause less damage than rattlesnake bites. The bite is often painless and not noticed for an hour or more. The first sign is usually a circle of red around the bite area.

If you're bitten by a venomous spider, you may notice any, or almost none, of the following as spider bites affect different people differently:

The brown recluse spider bite can become a dangerous wound if left unattended.

- Intense pain at the site of the wound
- Stiffness or joint pain
- Muscle spasms
- Abdominal pain, nausea, or vomiting
- Fever or chills
- Difficulty breathing or swallowing
- A wound that spreads or turns into a sore, an ulcerating sore if a brown recluse bite
- Dizziness
- Difficulty speaking
- Convulsions

Treatment of Venomous Spider Bites

- Wash the bite area with soap and water.
- Elevate the area to prevent spread of the venom.
- Tie a snug bandage above the area (if on an arm or leg) to further reduce spread of the venom, but do not make the bandage so tight that it impairs the blood circulation.
- Always seek immediate emergency medical care. An anti-venom medication is sometimes given for black widow spider bites. An anti-venom has not been approved for use on brown recluse victims as of this writing. In extreme cases hospitalization is required after black widow or brown recluse spider bites.

If possible, retrieve the spider and show EMTs so that it can be definitively identified.

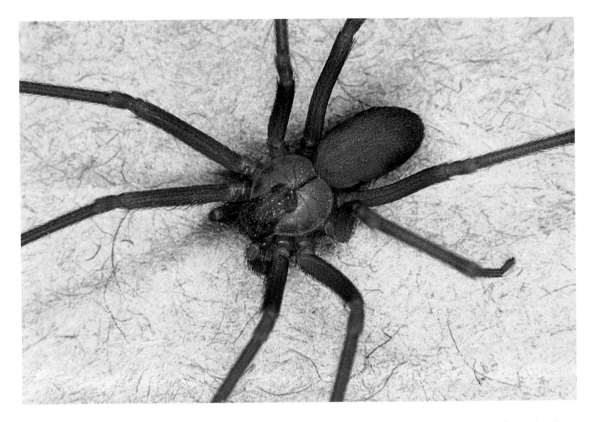

If you have a working cell phone, calling the Poison Control Center (twenty-four-hour hotline at 1-800-222-1222 in the US) allows you to reach toxicology experts who can work with you in establishing the proper diagnosis and management of a spider bite.

VENOMOUS SNAKEBITE

The proper treatment of a venomous snakebite has long been one of the most disputed subjects in the medical profession. Now most authorities agree that the following is the best action in the event of a venomous snakebite.

1. Get away from the snake quickly. It is not unusual for a snake to bite the victim repeatedly.
2. Identify the snake.
3. Calm the victim, and you remain calm. If snakebites are properly treated, the victims rarely die.
4. Immediately remove rings, bracelets, watches, shoes, or whatever from a bitten limb. The swelling will be fast, and such objects will constrict.
5. Keep the victim's activity to a minimum.
6. Take the victim to the nearest medical facility immediately. There is no field treatment, including cut and suck, that will do what emergency medicine in a hospital can do. This

situation is just one of many where getting found quickly is so important; it's up to you to set up contingency plans before you leave for the backcountry.

Other points to remember concerning snakebite:

Never give a snakebite victim alcohol. It speeds up the flow of blood through the system and hastens the effect of the bite.

Never use cryotherapy (ice), as this has been shown to be harmful to the snakebite victim.

It may be comforting to know that no venom, called a dry bite, is injected in 25 percent of all bites by poisonous snakes. However, absence of pain, swelling, or other symptoms does not necessarily mean that no venom has been injected. Bites that at first seem superficial can be fatal.

Most hospitals in snake country have antivenin for the treatment of snakebites. The odds are great that you will spend a lifetime outdoors and never be bitten or see a person bitten by a poisonous snake. However, the potential does exist and caution should be taken. Non-venomous snake bites can be painful and can have the resulting effects of infection. Know the identification of the snake and, if non-venomous, treat the wound as an open wound.

BLISTERS

Inspect your feet frequently for tender red patches, sometimes called hotspots, which are the beginnings of blisters. Treat a blister as soon as you notice it beginning. Cover these areas with

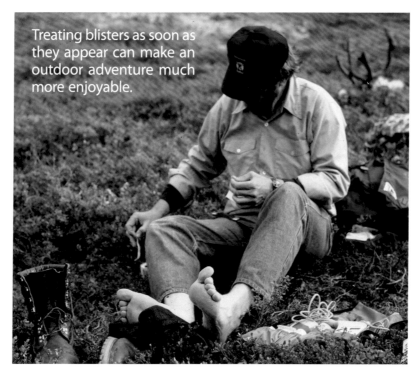

Treating blisters as soon as they appear can make an outdoor adventure much more enjoyable.

a gel pad, taped in place with an adhesive tape, to protect the skin from being rubbed by your footgear and forming a blister. Follow gel pad instructions.

Once a blister has formed, make a doughnut bandage—a round pad of moleskin with the center cut out—to protect it. Cleanse and re-bandage blisters daily.

It is best to not break blisters, because this increases the chance of infection and makes them more painful. However, if a blister must be drained, wash your hands thoroughly, cleanse the area around the edge of the blister and, with a sterilized needle, prick a tiny hole in the side of the swelling. Very gently ease the fluid out through the pinprick. When the blister is empty, cover the area with a sterile dressing, using adhesive tape.

To relieve pain and inflammation, soak the blistered area in hot water for twenty to thirty minutes, three or four times daily. After each soaking, cover the tender area with a sterile dressing.

The ragged dead skin of a broken blister should be trimmed carefully to prevent damaging new tissue, but should not be completely removed until the new skin has formed and toughened.

BURNS

Burns are usually classified by depth or degree of skin damage. Three general classifications are:

- First-degree. Redness, mild swelling, and pain.
- Second-degree. Deeper, with blisters appearing.
- Third-degree. Very deep burns which may look charred, with complete loss of all layers of skin.

Burns may also be described according to the extent of total body surface involved. For example, severe sunburn over much of the body, a first-degree burn, is considered serious and should receive prompt medical attention.

Treatment of burns is determined by these classifications.

First-degree burns

Use running water (preferably cold) or cloths soaked in ice water on the burned area to relieve pain. Applying After Burn to the burn can relieve pain. Dry sterile dressings may be used.

Second-degree burns

Use running water (preferably cold, but not ice water) or clean cloths wrung out in cold water until the pain subsides. Blot dry with sterile or clean cloth—not cotton balls because they stick—and apply sterile gauze or clean cloth as a dressing. Do not break blisters, remove shreds of tissue, or apply additional home medications. Treat for shock and obtain medical attention.

Third-degree (or deep second-degree) burns

Cover the burn to keep out air. This can be done with sterile dressings, freshly laundered clean sheets, or other linens. It is extremely important to treat for shock and to obtain advanced medical attention. Elevate the affected parts. Do not remove charred clothing that sticks to the burn. Do not apply cold water over the burn or apply home medications.

BLEEDING

You must control serious bleeding immediately!

Arterial Bleeding

Arteries carry blood away from the heart. Blood from a cut artery appears bright red and comes in distinct spurts that match the rhythm of the heartbeat. Arterial blood is under high pressure and a cut artery can result in the loss of a large volume of blood in a short period of time. Arterial bleeding must be controlled immediately or death may result.

Venous Bleeding

Veins carry blood back to the heart. Blood from a severed vein will appear dark red or bluish in color and will come in a steady flow. Venous bleeding is more easily controlled than arterial bleeding.

Capillary Bleeding

Bleeding from capillaries, small vessels that connect arteries and veins, commonly occurs as a result of small cuts and abrasions. Capillary bleeding is easily controlled.

Treatment

Direct Pressure

The most effective way to control external bleeding is direct pressure applied over the wound. The pressure must be firm enough to stop the blood flow and should be maintained long enough to close the damaged surface. Whenever possible, the bleeding part should be elevated above the level of the heart—for example, by raising a limb.

Pressure Dressing

If bleeding continues after pressure has been applied for about thirty minutes, you should apply a pressure dressing. This should be a thick dressing of gauze or other material applied directly over the wound and held in place by a tightly wrapped bandage. The bandage should not be so tight as to restrict circulation. Keep the dressing in place.

Tourniquet

Use a tourniquet in cases of massive wounds with severe bleeding or when direct pressure cannot control bleeding. A tourniquet should only be placed on upper leg or arms. Place a tourniquet between the wound and the heart, never directly over the injury or fracture. Use a stick to tighten the tourniquet just enough to stop the flow of blood. Bind the free end of the stick to the patient's limb. Cut-off blood flow can result in the loss of a limb. A lone survivor should not release the tourniquet. Under normal circumstances a tourniquet should be loosened every ten to fifteen minutes to restore blood flow to the limb, but this can be risky if you are by yourself.

WOUNDS

It is best to not try to close a wound in most survival situations. Leave the wound open to allow drainage from any infection that may occur. Cover the wound with a clean dressing and bandage and change the dressing daily if possible. In the case of a gaping wound, you can close the edges with a "butterfly" strip made from adhesive tape or a Band Aid.

SPRAINS

Sprains are the stretching or tearing of ligaments when a joint is twisted beyond its normal range of motion. Ice or some form of cold should be applied, if possible, to the injured area to reduce swelling. Heat should not be used since it will encourage internal capillary bleeding and increase swelling. A compression wrap, made by placing some form of padding over the injured joint and wrapping with an elastic bandage, will prevent swelling and give support. Where possible, the injured joint should be elevated above the level of the heart to reduce swelling.

FRACTURES

Relocating or setting bones will be difficult for a survivor. A simple fracture can be treated by immobilizing the injured limb with an improvised splint to reduce pain and prevent further injury. Fractures are best left to the attention of someone who is trained in advance or until help arrives. Just keep the victim as comfortable as possible until trained help arrives.

INSECT STINGS

Stings from wasps, hornets, bees, yellow jackets, fire ants, and so on are common during the summer. Unless there is a large number of stings, it is usually just an uncomfortable reminder to give these critters some space. However, if you happen to be a person who is allergic to insect stings, then a sting could put you into anaphylactic shock and be life-threatening. Wilderness travelers who know they are allergic to insect stings should talk to their doctor before an outing to get a treatment kit, usually an EpiPen for injecting a measured dose of epinephrine. This should be kept in their first aid kit and every member of the group should be told what it is for and how to use it.

A large number of stings can also be life-threatening. Use every caution to avoid these critters. Leave their homes alone and give them plenty of space.

When a bee stings someone, it often leaves its stinger with venom sac attached in the wound. It is best to scrape away the stinger with the edge of a knife blade, being careful not to squeeze the venom sac and force more venom into the wound.

On any sting, apply ice or cold water to the sting site to reduce pain and swelling. Applying After Bite or ammonia to the bite area also gives quick relief. I carry a tube of After Bite in my first aid kit.

TICK BITES

As we will discuss in Chapter 14 of this book, ticks are a threat to be taken seriously. While not all ticks carry diseases, many do, and their bites can introduce any one of a number of serious diseases to the victim. If you find a tick embedded in your body, it needs to be removed immediately. I carry tick removal forceps in my first aid kit. If you do a lot of warm weather outings, I suggest you do also.

The first rule when dealing with ticks is to use insect repellent on each warm-weather trip. Next is to do a daily tick check all over your body, at the end of the day, looking for embedded ticks. Some, such as deer ticks, are very small and will require a careful search to find them. Most important is to check those areas of the body that are somewhat hidden, such as the groin, armpits, folds of skin, navel, belt line, and head. Ticks like to hide in hairy, hidden, moist spots.

When you find a tick, here is how to remove it properly:

- Use tick removal forceps to remove a tick. If you don't have forceps, put on gloves or cover your hands with tissue paper, then use your fingers. Do not handle the tick with bare hands.
- Grab the tick as close to the embedded mouth as you can.
- Do not grab the tick around its swollen body. You could push infected fluid from the tick into your body if you squeeze it.
- Gently pull the tick straight out until its mouth lets go of your skin. Do not twist the tick. This may leave the head in your skin.

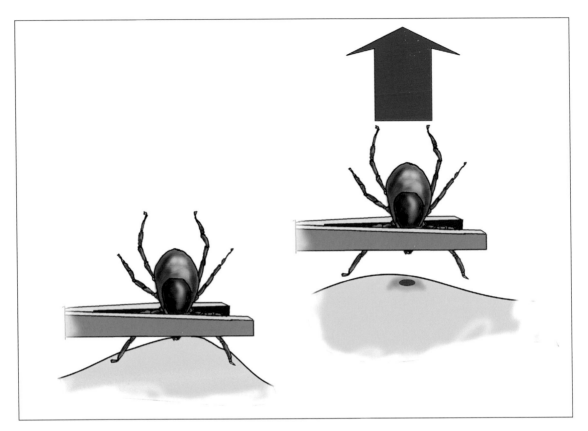

Tick Removal

- Put the tick in a tightly closed plastic bag and save it for later identification if needed.
- After the tick has been removed, wash the area of the tick bite with warm, clean water. Apply antiseptic to the bite. Be sure to wash your hands well with soap and water also.

SEEK OR CONSTRUCT A SHELTER

Shelter is defined as a "place affording protection from the elements." Every survivor, faced with the problem of protecting himself from the elements, must consider using every conceivable place already existing in his immediate area or using every available material at hand to improvise a place that will afford the protection that is needed. When deciding what type of shelter to build, you must first consider what the shelter is to protect you from, such as rain, wind, insects, heat, and cold. As an example, when in hot, arid areas, protection from the sun during the day may be the prime consideration. In frigid areas, retaining body heat or keeping out high winds may be what is called for. In some seasons, swarms of insects may be the factors that dictate what type of protection the survivor must seek.

In addition to protection from natural elements and conditions, an adequate shelter also provides the survivor with psychological well-being, so necessary for sound rest. Adequate rest is extremely important if the survivor is to make sound decisions, and the need for rest becomes more critical as time passes and rescue is prolonged. Some rest contributes to mental and physical health, and adequate shelter contributes to sound rest. Because of all these factors, adequate shelters must be placed high on the priority list if survival is to be successful.

Constructing shelter for your survival camp may or may not be a rush matter. If the weather is mild with no rain, you may postpone building a shelter. However, if the weather is bad or subject to being bad, then shelter construction may become very high on your list of priorities. One plus for shelter construction, assuming you are in good shape, is that it keeps you occupied. Constructing a good shelter where you can rest comfortably out of the elements takes time and some work, but this will help keep your mind off your troubles.

The location of your shelter site will depend on several things. The first priority is that it be in a location where search aircraft or ground parties can easily see you. I once led a ground search party looking for two lost hikers. It took us two days longer than it should have to find the hikers due to the hidden location they had selected to set up their survival camp.

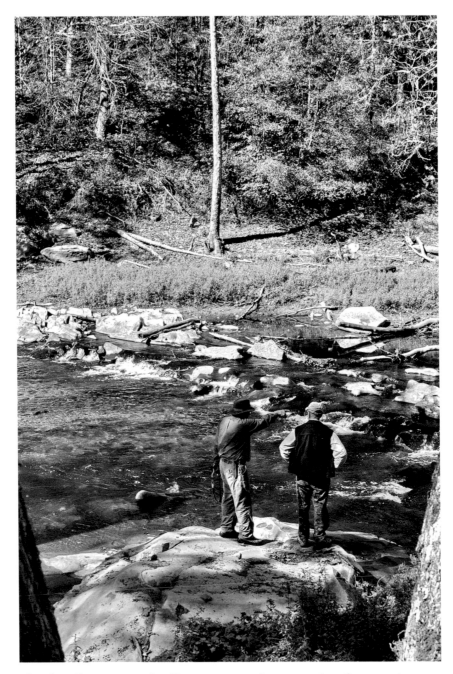

This fast-flowing creek offers water and an opening for searchers to spot the survivors; however, the survival camp should be located above the flash flood plain and far enough from the sound of the rushing waters so that aircraft or search parties can be heard.

If you are stranded with a vehicle, plane, boat, snowmobile, or canoe, try to either use the craft as a camp or set up your shelter nearby due to its high visibility. The exception would be if the craft were hidden by thick brush or trees.

If you are walking or skiing, select an open area, if possible, in which to set up your survival camp. This may require that you cut some brush or small trees. Avoid constructing your shelter in a low swamp area or in a dry creek bed. Your predicament is bad enough without having to contend with a flash flood or rising ground water. Also, mosquitoes may be a problem in warm weather.

Look up before selecting a shelter site. Don't build your shelter beneath standing dead trees or dead limbs or branches that are heavy with snow, as these could fall on you. Avoid thick overhead vegetation that could prevent aircraft from seeing your shelter or your distress signals. Avoid avalanche-prone slopes. Try to construct your shelter so that you can sleep reasonably comfortably. Select a level or near-level site. Remove stones and sticks. Your sleep is vital to conserve energy for survival.

Set up a ground-to-air signal as soon as you have a survival campsite selected. If the weather is not too bad, set your signals up before you construct your shelter. To wait may cause you to miss a chance for early rescue.

If possible, find an opening and set up your shelter near a source of water such as a spring, creek, river, or lake. This saves energy in getting water. Many times such an area is visited by man more frequently than other areas.

The type of shelter you select to use in your survival camp will be based on several factors.

1. What shelter material do you have with you—tube tent, vehicle, canoe, airplane, tarp, emergency blanket, sheet of plastic, etc.?
2. What equipment do you have to aid in shelter construction—ax, saw, knife, rope, multi-tool, etc.?
3. What natural materials are available for shelter construction—rocks, trees, poles, snow, cave, etc.?
4. What is the weather like now? What kind of weather do you expect?
5. What is the season of the year?

How effective your shelter will be will depend upon these factors, plus your ability to improvise and any previous training you have had in shelter construction.

NATURAL SHELTERS

The first rule in seeking shelter is to look around you to see if a natural shelter is already in existence that might save you time in setting up your survival camp.

A rock overhang or cave can make a good shelter. In fact, during the 1700s, the longhunters who were exploring the wilderness west of the Appalachian Mountains spent entire winters in survival-type camps they made under rock overhangs. By building up rock or log walls as windbreaks, these shelters can become comfortable. The downside is that due to their locations,

Reflector Fire

Lean-to using native materials

Lean-to made from natural materials gives some protection from the weather but few are watertight.

they are usually difficult to spot from the air or for any great distance on the ground, making rescue much more difficult. Locating ground-to-air signals nearby is a must when using these types of shelters.

In a mature forest, a huge tree that has a large hollow opening in the bottom can be used to get in out of the wind and weather. Unfortunately, not many forests that offer this type of temporary shelter exist any longer.

Many times freshly blown-down trees can be made into a survival shelter by cutting away the limbs near the ground. If large pieces of bark are around, use them to improve the roof.

If the blown-down tree has a huge root wad pulled up, and leaning over, it can be made into a shelter with little effort. However, since this shelter blends in with the surroundings, be sure to put out plenty of signals so that searchers will not overlook you.

An evergreen tree with low growing limbs that come out from the trunk and slope down to near the ground can be made into a shelter with some trimming. Again, this type of shelter blends in with the forest and really good ground-to-air signals and a fire are required for searchers to see you from the air.

If a quick search for natural shelters does not come up with an adequate shelter, then it will be up to the survivor to construct a man-made shelter from his survival kit.

TUBE TENTS

If you are traveling in the backcountry by foot, ATV, vehicle, plane, snowmobile, canoe, boat, horseback, or skis, you would be smart to take a tube tent with you. I learned while working in northern Canada and Alaska to always have a tube tent with me at all times. I have spent many unplanned nights in the wilderness. As mentioned earlier in this guidebook, the tube tent is easy and quick to set up. You simply run a rope or cords through the plastic tube and

Look for good natural shelter, such as this rock overhang. However, be sure you get out ground-to-air signals in an open area so the protected area can be seen from search aircraft.

tie it between two trees. Since they blow like a sail in high wind, it is a good idea to weigh down the front and rear openings with rocks or heavy logs until you get inside. Tube tents do a good job of keeping you dry in a rain or snow storm, they are excellent windbreaks, and due to their orange color they make a good signal.

Another feature I like about the tube tent is its use has little negative impact on the environment.

LEAN-TOS

A tarp, or emergency blanket, especially one in a metallic or bright orange color, is an extremely versatile shelter. It can be stretched over an open boat to make a cozy shelter. It can be stretched alongside an overturned canoe to form a lean-to. Stretch it from a wing of a plane to the ground or from the side of a vehicle to the ground. It makes a good lean-to, especially when trying to escape desert heat. A rain-proof lean-to is good in cold weather because, when used with a reflector fire, the shelter can be comfortable in the worst of weather.

EMERGENCY BLANKETS

The Mylar emergency blanket, which is sold in many camping supply stores or by online outdoor retailers, is a good item to carry in a personal survival kit. This blanket is made from a very thin but strong space-age material which can reflect 90 percent of the heat thrown against it. It is

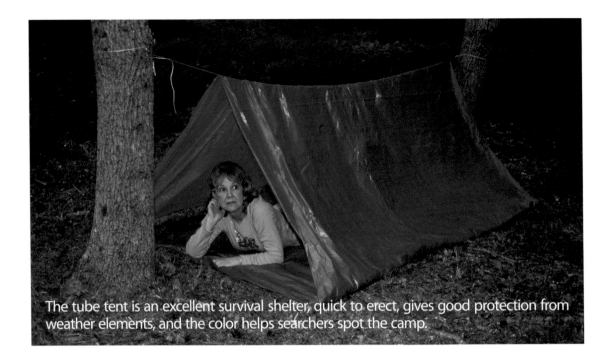

The tube tent is an excellent survival shelter, quick to erect, gives good protection from weather elements, and the color helps searchers spot the camp.

compact, about the size of a deck of playing cards. It can be made into a lean-to, and when used with a reflector fire, is very warm. This blanket makes a warm sleeping bag when folded properly.

Any type of plastic sheeting that is large enough can be made into a lean-to. This includes cutting large plastic garbage bags so that they make a square sheet.

WICKIUPS

In the arid southwestern United States, windbreaks and shade survival shelters called wickiups are made from brush. First, build a tripod using three poles that are ten to fifteen feet long apiece. Spread the legs of the tripod out six to eight feet. Next, stack long poles against the tripod until they take the shape of a tepee. Over these poles, place a thatching of sticks, grass, leaves, pine needles, evergreen boughs, and bark. These shelters are not usually rainproof but they can give good protection when a windbreak or shade is needed.

The wickiup is a good shelter to use in arid environments where shade during long hot days is important.

The emergency blanket can be made into a lean-to suitable for a quick survival shelter.

Since they blend in with the surroundings, be sure to put out plenty of signals so that searchers will not overlook you.

SNOW SHELTERS

In the winter, when there is snow on the ground, there are several survival shelters that can be constructed. However, shelters such as the well-known snow cave take a lot of energy and skill. The hole-in-the-snow shelter is one of the simpler shelters if the snow is at least four feet deep.

Hole-in-the-Snow Shelter

Find an evergreen tree having limbs extending down to snow level, then dig out all the snow around its trunk right down to the ground. Next, trim all the inside branches and use them to line the bottom and finish the top. Since this shelter is hidden, be sure to keep your ground-to-air signals out and clean of snow.

Snow Cave

A snow cave is an excellent cold-weather shelter, but it requires a lot of energy, a shovel or similar device, and some skill. Begin by finding a packed snowdrift that is about seven feet high and twelve feet or more wide. Packed snow is important so as to keep the roof of the snow cave rigid.

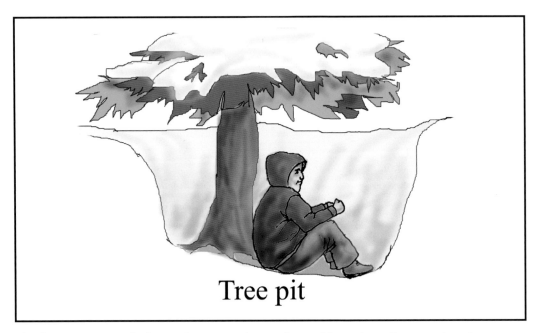

Tree pit

The hole in snow shelter is fast to make and provides a lot of protection; however, it requires effort to make sure the location can be spotted easily by searchers.

Snow trench

If getting out of the wind is a critical factor to survival, then a snow trench may be dug and blocks of packed snow used for a roof. This is usually a shelter of last resort and ground-to-air signals must maintained or the survivor may be overlooked.

While snow caves saves lives every year, they can take a lot of energy to construct and ground-to-air signals are a must.

Then start digging a low tunnel into the snow bank. After digging the tunnel two feet into the snow bank, hollow out an opening large enough for you to lie down.

Next, push a stick through the roof at a 45-degree angle to make a vent hole. In the back of the cave, build the bed platform some eighteen inches high. To conserve heat, the cave should be built just large enough to sleep, dress, and undress while lying in the sleeping bag. If desired, the sleeping shelf may be walled in to conserve heat. In addition to the ventilation hole through the roof, there should be another at the door.

Since they cannot be heated many degrees above freezing, life in snow shelters is rather rugged. It takes several weeks to acclimate yourself to the effects of living in such a cold atmosphere. You will require more food and hot drinks.

Regardless of how cold it may get outside, the temperature inside a small, well-constructed snow cave probably will not be lower than -10°F, and with a candle they can be heated to 32°F. Snow caves are difficult for searchers to find and the survivor probably will not be able to hear searchers if they are in the area.

Since snow shelters can blend in with the surroundings, good ground-to-air signals or brightly colored items laid out in an opening are a must.

There are many other crude shelters that can be made. The secret to shelter construction is simple: Use what is available to give yourself the protection necessary from the elements. Construct whatever shelter uses the least amount of energy and, if possible, keep it out where you can be seen. In most cases, the tube tent you carry in your survival kit is the best emergency shelter.

BUILD A SURVIVAL FIRE

You realize you are lost or, perhaps, stranded. You have stopped and calmed down. You have wisely decided to wait for rescue. Finding a nearby opening in the woods where your signals can be seen from the air, you take out your survival kit and locate your waterproof match container, and fire-starter, and build a fire. Sounds easy, doesn't it? But what if you didn't have matches? What if you didn't know how to build a fire? The unknowing might say you can always start a fire with flint and steel or with a fire drill or with a lens from your glasses. The unknowing might also say anybody can build a fire. How wrong this kind of thinking can be.

First, let's establish how valuable a fire can be to a lost or stranded person. Most people lost in the backcountry are scared, embarrassed, lonely, hungry, often cold or being attacked by flying pests, bored, and usually in poor spirits. A fire can solve many of these problems.

A survival fire serves many purposes:

- as a signal
- keeps the lost person busy
- drives away pests
- provides warmth
- purifies water
- dries clothing
- lifts spirits
- cooks food
- gives light
- may be used in crafting many useful items

Also, fire gives a sense of security and, in a way, provides company. Flame can harden a wooden spear point. Cooled down, the white ashes can be consumed to overcome constipation, the black ashes to stop diarrhea. In short, fire is one of the most valuable aids to your survival.

Fire serves many purposes in a survival camp. Safe and responsible firemaking should be one of the first survival skills learned.

The elements of fire making.

STEPS TO BUILDING A FIRE

Understand that you don't just start a fire, you build it. There are five things you need to build a fire successfully:

1. You must have oxygen, since burning is nothing more than rapid oxidation.
2. You must have a source of very hot heat, called an igniter. Matches, a flame from a butane lighter, hot sparks from a magnesium rod: All are igniters.
3. You must have tinder to catch the flame of the match, lighter, or sparks and start the fire.
4. Next, you will need kindling–small sticks and twigs to catch the fire from the tinder and get it going hotter.
5. Finally, you will need dry, dead fuel wood and a lot more of it than you will think. Dry, dead wood can be hard to find in wet weather but it is available on lower limbs of evergreen trees, standing dead timber, or by splitting wet logs or large limbs and getting to the dry wood interior.

Igniters

Matches

Except for a few experts, there are few among us who can start a fire without matches or a lighter. Flint and steel, bow drill, and fire plow all make interesting demonstrations but seldom work in a real survival camp.

Fresh wooden kitchen matches in a waterproof container are one of the best ways of starting a fire under survival conditions.

Also, they require the use of a lot of energy. Despite what many survival books say, there are few substitutes for fresh, dry, wooden strike-anywhere kitchen matches and prepackaged tinder in a real survival situation. Make it a practice to carry a waterproof match container supplied with a fresh supply of strike-anywhere kitchen matches and tinder with you in your survival kit at all times. This combination helps makes fire-starting in cold, wet, dark conditions much quicker and easier. Make sure you replace the matches every six months or so as matches will deteriorate and become useless.

As a backup, it is smart to carry a small butane lighter to use as a source of a flame. There have been times when I have seen butane lighters have their gas release button accidentally pushed in the survival kit so that when they are needed they would only spark. Also, they can fail to give a flame at high elevations. But when they work, they work well.

Starting a fire with a bow drill

Hand block

Spindle

Bow

Fireboard

The bow drill will, under ideal conditions, become an igniter, but contrary to what is often shown on TV, it is not an energy efficient means of having a survival fire. Add high humidity and wet wood and it is almost impossible.

Magnesium Rods

I also carry a high-quality four-inch magnesium rod that, with a little practice and good tinder, will start a fire as well as a match. To use the rod, you use the scraper blade that is attached to the rod, or your knife, to shave off thin pieces of magnesium into a pile, about the size of a quarter, into a nest of tinder. Keep the pile of shavings fluffy and not compacted. Scrape sparks from the rod onto the pile of shavings. When the sparks hit the shavings, a very hot white flame ignites the tinder. Add kindling and then increasingly larger sticks and pieces of wood as the fire grows. Practice starting a fire with your magnesium rod before you go into the field and have to use it.

Magnifying Lenses

Anyone who has used a magnifying lens to focus the sun's rays on his own skin remembers the sudden and unbearable hotspot produced. That same magnifier will make paper smoke quite quickly, charring it. But bringing real flames from the focused sun's rays requires some

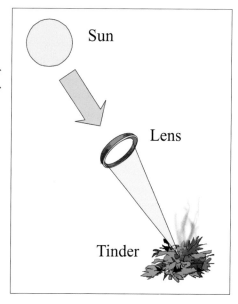

Sun

Lens

Tinder

Provided the sun is shining brightly, a fire may be started by using a lens from eyeglasses, camera, binoculars, etc.

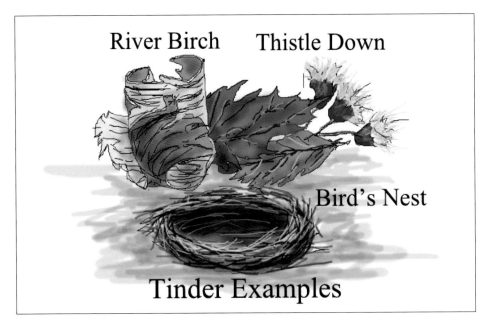

River Birch   Thistle Down

Bird's Nest

Tinder Examples

An example of three commonly found tinders.

practice with the lens you might use during a survival situation. And most important, this fire-starting method only works on sunny days.

Convex lens that you might use would include a camera lens, a plastic pocket magnifier, the front lens of a binocular or a pair of reading glasses. Before assuming that a lens will always get you a fire going on a sunny day in a survival crisis, experiment with different lenses on your chosen tinder at home first. Smoke is not enough. Practice until you can convert the sun's rays into a flame in the tinder. Once you have actually done this successfully a few times at home, then you will know what to expect in an emergency.

Batteries
Batteries found in planes, boats, automobiles, snowmobiles, ATVs, and other motors can give you enough spark, assuming they are charged, to get a fire going. Attach wires to each pole on the battery and scratch the ends together to produce sparks. Direct these sparks into the tinder.

Tinder
There are a lot of materials that can catch a spark or flame and burn easily. The trick is that you must have at least one with you or be able to identify and find natural tinder. Depending upon where you are, this can be difficult.

Here is some tinder that can be made to work. Some requires shredding, or pounding into powder:

- Shredded inner bark from cedar trees
- Shredded birch bark
- Crushed palm fiber
- Resinous sawdust
- Seed down from thistle or milkweed
- Dried pine needles, several years old
- Dried moss, such as goat's beard lichen
- 0000 steel wool
- Charred 100 percent cotton cloth
- Dry straw that is crushed
- Dry bird or rodent nest
- Crushed dead goldenrod
- Wild carrot tops
- Dryer lint
- Frayed rope
- Chaga fungus powder (inonotus obliquus)
- Dry cattail fuzz
- Cotton balls with petroleum jelly
- Crushed dried mullein leaves or coltsfoot
- Spruce tips, dried
- Dry powered conifer resin
- Crushed dried grass such as broom sedge

Here is how you can make your own fire-starting tinder from 100 percent cotton balls and petroleum jelly such as Vaseline Petroleum Jelly. I have used this tinder for years and it is dependable.

1. Place several 100 percent cotton balls in a plastic pail.
2. Put a tablespoon of petroleum jelly into the pail.
3. Mix the petroleum into the cotton balls with your hands until the balls are well coated.
4. Place balls into a plastic medicine container or a close-top bag for storage and carrying into field.
5. When ready to use, pull cotton ball apart and the thin strands will catch a spark or flame easily.

Note: Handling the cotton balls is a little messy.

Ingredients for making tinder from 100 percent cotton balls and petroleum jelly.

Kindling

Kindling is readily combustible fuel that is added to tinder as soon as there is sufficient flame to ignite it. Add kindling to tinder to bring the burning temperature up to the point where larger and perhaps less combustible fuel can be added. When you think "kindling," think small, from the size of a match stick to the size of your thumb, and no more than twenty-four inches in length. Use a small hatchet or ax to split dry large sticks of wood into small pieces for kindling. Split kindling or fuel wood burns more readily than round wood. Here are common materials used for kindling:

- Small dry twigs or plant fibers
- Wood such as logs, large limbs, etc. split to small size
- Heavy cardboard
- Wood pieces removed from the inside of larger pieces, especially during wet conditions
- Dry wood that has been soaked in or doused with a highly flammable material such as kerosene, oil, or wax. Use with caution!
- Small dead branches, still attached to conifer trees, near the ground, called squaw wood in the far north
- Fuzz stick used to get other kindling going
- Candle; blow-out-proof birthday candle is good in the wind. Use it to get other kindling going.

Kindling should be small material that is very dry and has a high combustible point. It should be arranged over the tinder in such a fashion that it ignites when the flame from the tinder reaches it. Once on fire, the kindling burns hot enough to ignite the larger fuel wood above it. When you gather kindling, gather a generous supply, especially in wet weather, and go to great lengths to keep it dry. It usually takes a lot more kindling than you think to get a survival fire going.

Fuel

Fuel consists of those large pieces of wood or other material that keep the fire burning for long periods and may be any of the following:

- Dry standing deadwood and dry dead branches. Deadwood is easy to split and reduce to short sections by using a hatchet, ax, or pounding it on a rock.
- The inside of fallen tree trunks and large branches. These may be dry even if the outside is wet. Use the heart of the wood.
- In treeless areas, you can find other natural fuels, such as dry grass, which you can twist into bunches; peat dry enough to burn (found at the top of undercut banks); dried animal dung; animal fats; and sometimes, though rare, even natural deposits of coal.
- Even green or wet wood can be used for fuel if you have a hot enough bed of kindling burning. This hot fire forces the moisture out of this fuel and gets it hot enough to ignite. Caution: Highly flammable liquids should not be poured on any fire, even smoldering ashes, as they can explode into a ball of fire, causing serious injuries.

- Gather soft woods for flames for quick heating, hard woods for long-lasting coals such as needed for cooking or keeping warm all night.
- Gather three times more fuel wood than you think you will need.
- Keep your supply of fuel wood and kindling dry. If you don't have a tarp or other waterproof cover, use bark, large leaves, flat rocks, or anything that will shield this precious resource from rain and melting snow.
- Damp wood should be placed near the campfire to dry and store for future use.
- Remember that a campfire burns downwind, so add fuel on the lee side.
- Building a fire in the first attempt requires practice and thought. Many try to add large pieces of wood too quickly. Others try to pile on so much wood that the flame gets too little oxygen to burn. Still others do not gather up the different sizes of wood necessary to build a fire in advance, and the fire goes out while they are running around trying to find the tinder, small sticks, and fuel wood necessary.
- If you expect search planes, or are in a position so that ground searchers might see your fire or smoke, keep plenty of kindling and fuel wood on hand to get a fire going again quickly for signaling. Also, during the day, keep some green or wet leaves or conifer boughs on hand to create a signal smoke quickly.
- If you must build a fire for survival, select a location where the fire is safe and has a minimum impact on the environment.

Can you really build a fire with one match when you are cold, shaking, wet, tired, and scared? Practice, practice, practice at home! This is the time to master the art, not when it really counts.

SIGNAL FOR HELP

Whether you are lost or stranded, the first step to being found is to leave a trip plan with a responsible person. Next, you need to be seen or heard. Assuming you have let someone know where you are going and when you expect to return, someone will soon be looking for you in the area in which you are located. Your first concern should be to get prepared to be seen, or heard, by the rescue party.

Try to avoid making your survival camp near a waterfall or roaring creek. You need to be where you can hear searchers, and a survival camp in these types of locations drowns out sounds made by searchers and sometimes your signals to them.

Signaling is a survival skill that no one should take lightly, especially since we now have excellent search aircraft that can be in the air over the search area soon after a person is reported missing. Also, hasty teams of experienced searchers can be on the ground looking for a missing person within a few hours after he or she is reported missing.

Here are some of the best signaling methods, second only to a working cell phone.

SIGNAL MIRROR

Most survival experts consider the signal mirror to be one of the best signal devices available, especially when aircraft are used in a search. They are small and easy to carry in a survival kit, coat, or daypack. It amazes people how far a reflection from these little mirrors can be seen.

US Air Force rescue planes have spotted a signal mirror from as far away as one hundred miles. Distances of thirty to forty miles are common. Several times lost people have used a signal mirror to attract the attention of rangers in a forest fire tower, or searchers miles away on a mountainside or in a flat desert.

A Texas pilot was flying home from Alaska when his helicopter crashed in a thick spruce forest in British Columbia. He survived for fourteen days at the crash site. He was found because he used a piece of shiny metal as a signal mirror to get the attention of a search-and-rescue plane as

73

A CD makes an excellent signal mirror, complete with aiming hole in center.

it flew over. Many downed combat pilots and military special ops units in Southeast Asia, during the 1960s and 1970s, owe their lives to signal mirrors.

Signal mirrors may be purchased at outdoor supply stores and websites. Most signal mirrors are made from glass or tough plastic and have instructions on the back. While the instructions are easy follow, no one should wait until they get in a survival situation before learning how to use the mirror properly. Practice until you understand the correct way to use the mirror.

Most signal mirrors have a hole in the center for aiming. They are used to reflect the sun, moon, or aircraft searchlight to signal an overhead aircraft, boat, or other target such as a search party that is within view but a long distance away.

Here is how to use the signal mirror:

1. Hold the mirror in front of your eye so you can see through the hole.
2. Make sure the shiny side is toward the sun, moon, or searchlight.
3. Take your other hand and hold it out at arm's length.
4. Reflect light from the sun, moon, or searchlight onto the extended hand.
5. While watching through the aiming hole, turn the mirror in order to swing the reflected spot toward the target.
6. Keep your signal mirror with you and be prepared to use it fast.

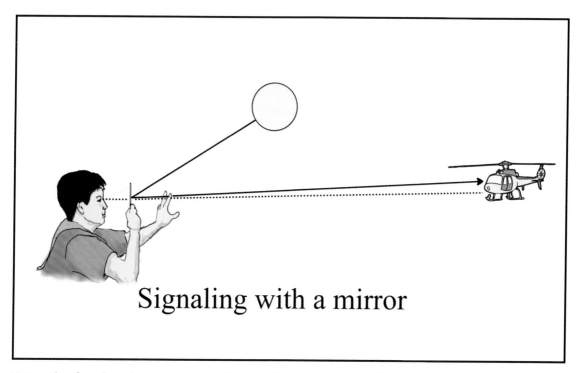

Signaling with a mirror

Using the free hand as a sight use it to guide the mirror reflection to the aircraft.

Signal mirrors may be improvised from almost any shiny object, aluminum foil, ladies' compact mirror, car mirror, top of an aluminum can with a hole in the center, or even a CD disk. In fact, a CD makes an excellent signal mirror, due to its highly reflective surface and to the hole in the center being used for an aiming device.

Signal mirrors work best on bright sunny days, but they also work on hazy and cloudy days, on bright moonlit nights, and when searchlights are used by boats or aircraft.

The combination of flash from the signal mirror, the bright color of the tube tent, and the bright color from the coat makes this lost hunter easy to spot from the air.

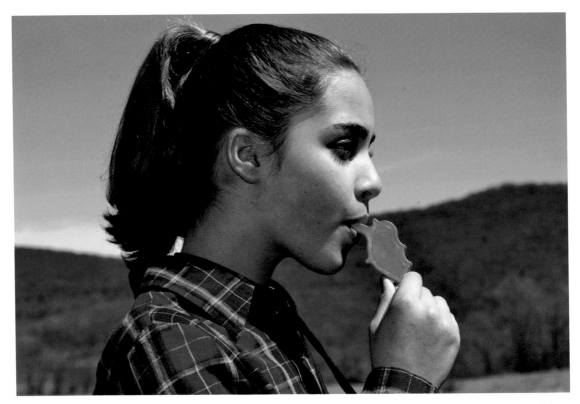

A sound from a quality whistle will carry much further than the human voice and last much longer.

WHISTLES

Loud, high-quality whistles used by military, police, and sports coaches make excellent signal devices. They are easy to carry, require little energy to use, and, at up to 130 decibels, they can be heard much farther than the human voice and last long after a shouting person becomes hoarse. Whistles make good signals when a ground party is conducting the search. They are easily heard and, if tracking dogs are being used, they can hear whistles from great distances. Be sure to get a whistle in a bright orange or yellow color, so it can be found quickly and easily when needed.

In a survival situation, take the whistle from the survival kit and wear it around your neck on a cord so that it is ready for immediate use if a search team is detected.

To use a whistle effectively, stay calm and do not blow on it until you think that someone is within hearing distance. To blow a whistle continuously for hours when no one is around only wastes vital energy and brings on frustration. When you think enough time has gone by and people are likely looking for you, try giving a few blows on your whistle every thirty minutes just in case someone is out there, and then whistle them in. When you hear searchers, stay put and let them come to you.

FIRES

One of the best-known signals, both day and night, is a fire. At night, a bright campfire in an opening can be seen for miles from the air and a fair distance on the ground, especially in mountains. During the day, the same fire can be made to smoke when wet leaves or green vegetation is piled on it. Smoke during the day is an excellent signal.

Remember to be extremely careful when making and using a signal fire. When in a survival situation, most people are upset, excited, and mistakes happen easily. You are in enough trouble already without getting caught in a forest fire that you set.

Carry kitchen matches in a waterproof container and fire-starting tinder with you. Know how to start a fire even in wet conditions. Building a fire in a survival situation is more difficult than most people think. Master the skill of fire-making before you actually need it.

For a fire to be effective, it must be prepared before the time that a rescue aircraft or search team enters the area. Then you only need to light it quickly and the fire does the rest. You should supplement the fire with other forms of signaling.

FLASHLIGHTS

One of the new generations of ultra-bright LED flashlights makes an excellent signal at night. If the flashlight has an on-off switch that allows you to signal SOS in Morse code, so much the better. Three short flashes, three long flashes, and three short flashes are the SOS signal that is known to all rescue personnel. Even a small light out in the open can be seen a long way by aircraft at night.

BRIGHT CLOTHING AND EQUIPMENT

The bright-orange clothing that many hunters wear works well as a signal, especially if aircraft are used in a search. Even a white T-shirt or yellow rainsuit can be used as a signal panel. Brightly colored equipment such as a red tube tent or orange pack can also be used to signal searchers.

GROUND-TO-AIR SIGNALS

Search pilots are all familiar with ground-to-air signals. These are large symbols the lost or stranded person forms out in the open, where they can be seen by search aircraft. They must contrast with the ground to be seen. Dark limbs on snow or light-colored rocks on dark soil are examples of what has worked.

The signal symbol must be large to be seen from the air. For example, the "X," the universal signal for help, ideally should have legs that are three feet wide and eighteen feet long.

GUNSHOTS

Gunshots can be good signals and they carry a long distance, although they must be used at the right time to be effective. If you are in trouble during hunting season, your random shots may be mistaken as shots from hunters. Save your ammunition and wait until well after dark. Then fire three shots into the air. Listen for three shots in return. If you make contact, from that point on fire only one shot when you hear your searchers shoot. Save your ammo, as it may take several shots to guide them in.

GROUND - TO - AIR SIGNALS

X	UNABLE TO TRAVEL
↑	AM TRAVELING IN THIS DIRECTION
I	NEED DOCTOR - EMERGENCY
II	NEED MEDICAL SUPPLIES
F	NEED FOOD AND WATER
⋁	NEED GUN AND AMMO
□	NEED MAP AND COMPASS
Y	YES
N	NO
⌐⌐	DO NOT UNDERSTAND MESSAGE
LL	ALL WELL
K	WHICH DIRECTION SHOULD I GO?

Ground-to-air signals recognized by aircraft pilots.

  THE SCOUTING GUIDE TO SURVIVAL

SHADOW SIGNALS

In open snow-covered plains, it is often difficult to find materials to make ground-to-air signals or SOS. If this is the case, build your ground-to-air signal out of mounds of snow so that they cast a shadow. Due to the lack of contrast, it is the shadow the pilot or spotters will see from the search aircraft. To be effective, these shadow signals must be oriented to the sun to produce the best shadow possible. Usually an east-west line gives best results. In this case, other signal devices should be used in earnest at the same time.

Several years ago a thirteen-year-old cross-country skier who spent the night on a mountain during a sudden snowstorm was found unharmed after a ski resort employee saw a giant SOS the youngster had stamped in the snow. It was the shadows in the SOS depression that made the signal stand out.

The most important factors about signals are that you know how to use them properly, and that you have the signals ready for use on a short notice. Also, it is important that you choose an open area to do your signaling. Many of the signals discussed will not be seen from the air if you sit under a thick canopy of tall trees to await rescue. Select an open area, if possible, to wait for your rescuers and have your signals ready. Areas such as old roads, fields, sites of old forest fires, sea or lake shores, or any other types of openings will help you be seen early in the search. Remember to stay where you are, and don't give in to the urge to travel. Signaling will bring help to you.

An actual photo of where ground-to-air signals led to an arctic rescue.

11

SAFE WATER IS ESSENTIAL

There once was a time when it would have been unnecessary to include a chapter in this book on how to make water found in the backcountry safe for drinking, but those days are gone. Today there are few areas left in the backcountry, or anywhere else, where one can trust the quality of

Unfortunately no creek in today's world can be considered a source of safe drinking water before the water drawn is treated or filtered.

the water and be safe in doing so. Therefore, it behooves every backcountry traveler to learn the skill of making water safe for drinking, especially those who might possibly face a survival emergency.

Survival is a stressful period in a person's life, and the need for pure drinking water is important. The body is approximately 75 percent water, and the intake and output of liquids are necessary for normal functions of the vital organs.

Daily water requirements, a minimum of two quarts, help maintain proper balance and efficiency within the system of the body. During cold weather, breathing alone releases a lot of moisture from the body. Perspiration also releases moisture. Any lower intake of water results in gradual dehydration and the loss of the body's efficiency. Losing water to the extent of 2.5 percent of body weight, or approximately one and one-half quarts of body water, will reduce efficiency 25 percent. This loss could be deadly in a survival emergency.

Several commercial tablets such as Potable Aqua fit easily into a survival kit and make most waters safe to drink.

There are many myths about water purifying itself in the outdoors. One popular theory is that water, swiftly running over, around, and through rocks purifies itself. Do not believe it. This is not a valid hypothesis. Another myth claims that if clear water sits in the sun for an hour, the germs are killed. Again, this is untrue. Nature produces clean water, but once it becomes unclean, rarely does nature clean it again. It is your responsibility to treat questionable water.

Never trust water from an unknown source. If you do not know the source of your water supply, do not trust it. Some of the diseases you may contract by drinking impure water include dysentery, giardiasis, cholera, and typhoid. The best way to be assured of having safe water is to carry enough with you to use for drinking. However, in an unexpected survival situation of several days, this is not always possible. It is on these types of emergencies that water treatment knowledge is a must. Here are several methods for treating questionable water:

BOILING

One of the best methods for treating water is the boiling method. Boiling water for ten minutes will produce germ-free water for drinking or cooking. Since boiling leaves water with a flat taste, you should pour it back and forth between two containers several times once it has cooled. This aerates it, giving back its natural taste. A vessel for boiling water can be formed from the aluminum foil in your survival kit.

COMMERCIAL TABLETS

Drugstores and outfitter stores usually have halazone tablets or Potable Aqua tablets for the treatment of water. A bottle of the tablets fits nicely in the individual survival kit. Both do excellent jobs. Halazone tablets have been used successfully for years. Add two tablets to a quart of water and follow with a thirty-minute wait. The newer product, Potable Aqua, requires one tablet to a quart of water, capping loosely to allow a little leakage. Wait three minutes and shake thoroughly. Wait thirty minutes before drinking. If the water is very cold or contains rotten leaves or silt, use two tablets. You can use the gallon re-sealable plastic bag in which your survival items are packed for a water container. The plastic bag in which the tube tent is packed also makes a good water container.

IODINE TREATMENT

While iodine is no longer used in some of the newer first aid kits, it is still in older kits and makes a good water treatment. Simply add five drops of iodine to one quart of clear water and ten drops to cloudy water. Let water stand for thirty minutes before drinking.

At this point I should point out that any time you are treating water in a canteen, jug, or other type of container, you should be sure to rinse the cap, spout, screw threads, and lid with some of the treated water. You do not want to miss treating any surface that may come into contact with your mouth or the water you are drinking.

WATER FILTERING DEVICES

There are a number of compact water filtration units such as Sawyer and LifeStraw that can give the backcountry traveler safe water. They have been proven to filter out Giardia and other harmful threats, and the units fit into a pack easily.

GETTING WATER IN EXTREME COLD CONDITIONS

Dehydration is almost as great a problem in cold conditions as in the desert, because all the water is frozen into snow or ice. Some streams or lakes may provide access to flowing water (but be very careful not to fall into the water). If the sun is shining, you can melt snow on a dark plastic bag or tarp, flat rock, or any surface that will absorb the sun's heat. Arrange the surface so that the melted water will drain into a hollow depression or container.

Anyone traveling under frigid conditions should carry a small portable gas-type stove and pot for melting ice or snow. Whenever possible, melt

Compact water filtration systems, such as this LifeStraw, offer the backcountry traveler an option to carry in their survival kit.

ice rather than snow because ice yields more water for the volume with less heat and time. Snow is seventeen parts air and one part water. If you melt snow by heating, put in a little snow at a time and compress it, or the pot will burn. If water is available, put a little in the bottom of the pot to protect the pot and add snow gradually.

When melted, glacial ice gives roughly twice the water, per fuel unit, in half the time that snow does. In addition, snow is more likely to contain dirt, soot, and animal and human contaminants.

Don't try to eat ice or snow. A day or two of taking water in this manner will make the mucous membrane of your mouth so swollen and raw as to prevent eating or drinking until the inflammation subsides. Also, your body gives up heat to melt the snow. Dogs eat snow and get away with it; humans can't.

Once you have water, give it the boiling treatment.

COLLECTING RAIN AND DEW FOR DRINKING WATER

Dew sometimes forms on metal auto hoods and airplane wings, tube tents, or on plant leaves that can be sponged with a cloth. Some water can be obtained as dewdrops on the underside of a plastic sheet spread on the ground during the night. Use every possible means of water conservation and keep supplementing your water supply.

Watch the weather signs and be ready to collect rainwater. Rub wax from candles or butter to waterproof fabric for collecting rainwater. Spread out your waterproofed clothes to catch the rain. Remember that large leaves, holes in tree trunks, and depressions in rocks will collect water

A solar still can be made in arid environments to gather small amounts of water for drinking. It does require you carry the necessary ingredients with you to make a solar still and the amount of water obtained is usually small.

for you also. Dig a hole in the ground and line it with cloth, canvas, plastic, oiled paper, or leaves–anything to stop rapid drainage into the earth.

Rainwater can be diverted from leaning trees and branches by a long cloth wick (torn from any cloth) leading into a container.

GETTING SEDIMENT OUT OF WATER

If clear water is not available, take the following steps:

1. Filter the water to be treated through a clean handkerchief or similar fabric.
2. Let the filtered water stand until any remaining sediment has settled to the bottom.
3. Pour off the clear water into the vessel; treat the water.

12

FOOD: NOT A NECESSITY

Every time the subject of survival is brought up, the first discussions usually revolve around edible wild foods and how to procure them. We are obsessed with eating. It has been proven many times that most of us can go without eating several weeks, if necessary, and not die. Most of us carry around an abundance of fat that could keep us alive for a long period of time. For this reason, and the fact that this book was written for the most likely survival scenario, not more than seventy-two hours in the woods, we will not cover the many edible wild plants and animals that are available in North America.

EDIBLE WILD PLANTS

For those who think they cannot go for three days without eating three meals a day, I would suggest they read and study the many survival books and other books which describe and show detail photos of the approximately two thousand edible wild plants and seven hundred toxic wild plants found in North America. Distinguishing one from the other requires a lot of field experience during all four seasons. A book like this cannot scratch the surface on this subject. A book that does is the *Scouting Guide to Foraging*, also available from Skyhorse Publishing.

WILD PLANT EDIBILITY TEST

If for some reason you are in a situation where there are wild plants you think you must eat but don't know which ones are edible, the US Air Force Survival School Edibility Test may be of some help:

1. Never use mushrooms or fungi.
2. Poisonous plant life means all parts, including flowers, can be toxic. Use caution with plants having these characteristics:
   - Milky or discolored sap
   - Spines or fine hairs
   - Bitter or soapy taste

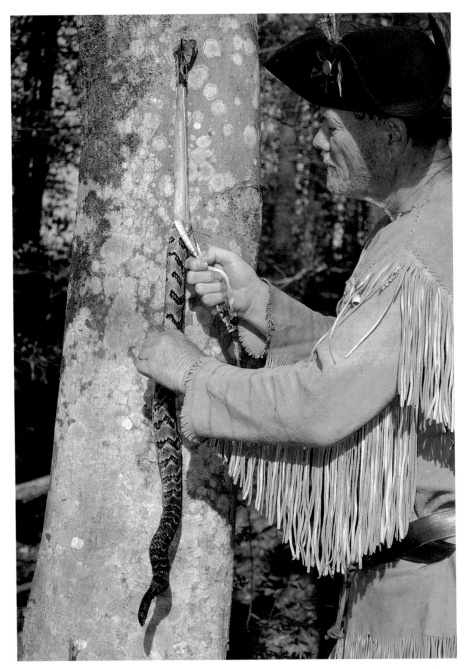

While mountain men could live off the land for months at a time, few among us today have those skills. Since the majority of lost or stranded people are found within seventy-two hours, starvation is not a likely threat.

- Beans or bulbs
- White or red berries
- Shiny leaves
- Umbrella flowers

3. Take a small mouthful and chew it. Wait five minutes for any effects such as burning, stinging, or numbing.
4. If there is none, swallow and wait eight hours for any effects such as diarrhea, cramps, pain, numbing, or vomiting.
5. If there is none, repeat the process, using a handful of the plant, and wait another eight hours for ill effects.
6. If none, the plant is considered safe to eat.

Keep in mind that any new or strange food should be eaten with restraint until the body system has become accustomed to it. Also, don't expect wild plants to taste good. Many don't, and others are almost tasteless. It takes some adjusting to get your stomach to accept a diet of wild plants.

Some other things you need to know about wild plants:

1. Plants you see animals eating may be toxic to man. Deer love poison ivy, for example.
2. Plants that you may eat in one stage may not be edible in other stages of growth. Pokeweed is a good example of this.
3. Some parts of plants may be edible while others may not be. Wild plum is an example of this.

EDIBLE WILD ANIMALS

If the survivor really must resort to wild foods in order not to starve to death, then wild animals may be a better choice than wild plants, if he or she has hunting or trapping skills. North America has a good population of wild animals, both large and small, that are edible. The trick is that you first must get them before you can cook them. Even the Lewis and Clark Expedition members, at one point, almost starved to death due to not killing any game to eat, and had to depend upon roots.

Depending upon the time of year and where you are geographically, there is some form of animal that you can eat if you can get it. Insects and small aquatic animals may be the easiest to gather and highest in protein, but what if it is winter? There may be an abundance of larger animals, but if you lack the skills necessary to kill the animals, you can go hungry. And remember, animals are often hard to find even by the most skilled hunters. Provided you can kill them, wild animals are a good source of food and may be cooked over the survival fire with ease. Just don't expect them to taste like home cooking.

Survival food is not an important need for the short term. Shelter and signaling are. Accept the fact that the last thing you should concern yourself with is the procurement of food. If you have filed a trip plan with a responsible person and you stopped just as soon as you knew you were in trouble, you will be rescued long before your hunger pains become serious. Think of this experience as the beginning of that diet you have been considering.

13

IMPORTANCE OF GETTING SLEEP

Sleeping warm and comfortably cannot be emphasized enough in the survival emergency. You need a lot of energy for the tasks at hand, and the mind needs to be sharper than during your normal day-to-day life, as the decisions you make will determine your well-being and the outcome of your situation.

If you have a tube tent and emergency sleeping bag in your survival kit and set up the tube tent so that you can get into the bag before you get wet, then chances are good you will sleep warm. How well you clean the tube tent site will determine how comfortably you sleep. Remember you do not have an air mattress or anything else thick between you and the ground. A few minutes spent removing stones, sticks, and other debris and laying down a bed of dry leaves can make the difference between an uncomfortable night and a comfortable one.

But what about a night spent without the aid of a tube tent or emergency sleeping bag? In this case there are several options, depending upon the terrain where you determine to camp. The first rule is to get into a shelter of some type that can give you protection from the rain, snow, or wind; if the shelter is conducive to having a fire, so much the better. Your chances of actually getting some sleep improve when you can stay warm. Be sure to gather three times as much wood as you think you will need, as it will probably take it to keep the fire going all night. It is difficult to keep the body warm or to get enough sleep when you must make two or three trips out into the cold darkness to gather up fuel wood.

The ideal sleeping shelter, aside from the tube tent/emergency sleeping bag combination, is the well-made lean-to with its back to the wind and a reflector fire directing heat into the shelter. Using a sheet of aluminum foil, a wall of green limbs, rocks, and so on as a reflector, the all-night fire can keep a lean-to reasonably warm throughout the night as long as there is enough fuel wood. As the fire dies down, you simply toss on enough wood to keep it going another few hours.

When rain or snow is not a threat, a reflector fire directing heat to a large rock or dirt bank, blocking the wind, can make a nice place to sleep. The heat is reflected to the rock or bank and back onto you while you sleep. You have heat from two sides.

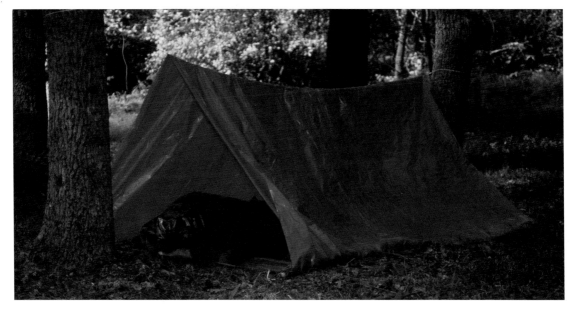

Getting a restful night's sleep is essential to keeping the mind sharp. This will help you make good decisions towards being rescued.

You can build a fire on the spot you plan on sleeping and let it warm up the earth for a few hours, then rack the fire away to a new spot and sleep on the warm earth. If you have a means of digging, you can dig a shallow hole where your body is going to lie, shovel in a bed of hot ashes, and cover it with a layer of soil. Make sure to cover all the ashes and give it a "try and see" test. If you have enough cover soil on, you will have a bed that's not too hot or too cold. This is an energy-consuming means of having a warm bed.

Some experienced backwoodsmen heat a number of flat rocks and place them on the ground. Next they place a thick layer of precut evergreen boughs over the rocks and sleep on them. Again, this type of warm sleeping requires a lot of energy and experience.

If you don't have an emergency bag, sleeping bag, or blanket, you can use dry dead grass, leaves, or evergreen boughs to give you some protection from the cold. Remember that insulation is dead air space and anything that will create dead air space will help keep you warm. The rainsuit can offer a lot of warmth when sleeping due to its ability to stop the wind. By stuffing dead, dry grass or leaves inside the rainsuit, you can also make a makeshift sleeping bag. Be resourceful.

Here are some tips for getting a good night's sleep:

- Take the time to make the bed site as level and soft as possible.
- Be sure to use every windbreak available.
- Gather three times as much firewood as you will think you need.
- Eat sweets just before bedtime, if you have them, to boost your metabolism.

- Do not lie awake the first night expecting searchers every minute. You will hear them if they get close and you will need to be rested the next day.
- At night, due to your situation, your senses will be acutely aware and you will hear every noise. Remember there is nothing out there that will hurt you.
- When sleeping with your clothing on, keep everything loose, including boots. The better circulation you have, the warmer you will sleep. This also permits moisture to evaporate.

You can bet that even in the best of circumstances you are not going to sleep in the survival camp as well as you do at home, but with a little care you can get some sleep and that rest is most important to getting found.

DEALING WITH INSECTS AND SPIDERS

Few things can ruin an outdoor adventure faster than hordes of mosquitoes and/or blackflies. In large numbers, they have been known to bring armies to a halt, stampede animals, and turn countless camping trips into horror stories. In a stranded or lost emergency, they can become very dangerous. Even in cold areas, a sudden warm snap can bring out the pests in numbers.

Of the more than 1,600 varieties of mosquitoes, 120 are found in the North America. Many of these are known to transmit such diseases as West Nile virus, encephalitis, and dengue fever. Just their bites alone, in high numbers, are very dangerous.

Nuisance bugs are a part of many outdoor trips, but with a little planning, and preventive measures, they will not spoil the fun of the trip. Here are some ways to keep your encounters with these "critters" to a minimum.

- Cool weather sends these insects away, so when practical, plan your outdoor trip in cold weather.
- Call ahead and find out if the area you are going into has any potential nuisance bug activity during the time you will be visiting. If so, find out what and plan preventive measures.
- If you are going into an area with a pest you have no experience with, take the time to know how to avoid or repel them. Say you are from the North and have never encountered fire ants. Go to a little trouble and learn how to recognize their mounds. If you are forced to wade in flooded areas, know that fire ants survive floods by forming a ball as large as a basketball and floating to dry ground. You don't want your fishing waders to be the dry spot they rub up against.
- Black widow and brown recluse spiders usually stay hidden, so when in their areas, be safe by shaking out your clothing and footwear before putting them on and by not putting your hands into secluded areas when you're out in the woods. When using outhouses, always check under the seat, a favorite home range for black widows.

- Chiggers thrive in heavy vegetation, so during warm weather, don't get into thick vines and leaves. This helps avoid ticks as well.
- For repelling ticks, chiggers, deer flies, and horse flies, spray your clothing with permethrin-based repellent. Apply a Deet-based repellent to your exposed skin. Deet-based repellents last only a few hours, whereas permethrin-based repellents applied only to clothing last for several days. Be sure to read the labels of each product and follow the instructions.
- Stinging insects such as hornets, bees, and yellow jackets usually only require that you give their nests a wide berth. In the fall, bees and yellow jackets will often come to your picnic lunch and you will have to use more caution at that time.
- Mosquitoes and blackflies can be kept at bay by using a Deet-based repellent or by using the very effective Thermacell repellent appliance. Keeping exposed skin to a minimum, such as using a head net and taping sleeves and pant legs closed, also helps keeps the blood-sucking damage to a minimum.

Insects are a valuable part of the outdoor world, and with a little knowledge, planning, and repellent, we can share the outdoors with them without suffering.

To deal with these flying pests, we need to know more about them.

MOSQUITOES

Mosquitoes mature in standing water. It is the female mosquito that causes us grief, as she needs a high-protein meal before she is able to lay her eggs. Physiological restrictions make it impossible for her to eat anything which is not in liquid form, and the handiest liquid, high-protein meal available to her is blood. The male mosquito is a vegetarian and feeds on plant and fruit nectar.

Sensors, which are attracted to warm, moist animals, help the female mosquito locate a meal. The generally accepted theory in the scientific community is that the mosquito finds its victim by identifying and following carbon dioxide and lactic acid in the air. Lactic acid is produced by muscle movement, and carbon dioxide is given off when we breathe.

Once she finds a victim, she penetrates the victim's skin with a hollow, flexible snout, called a proboscis, and feeds. The itch and local swelling around the "bite" is an allergic reaction to the mosquito's saliva, which contains an anticoagulant to facilitate the flow of blood.

BLACKFLIES

For those who have been bitten by blackflies, the bite is a form of torture. These small, humpbacked flies have few equals when it comes to inflicting pain. Of over three hundred varieties of blackflies in the world, North America has been cursed with at least fifty of them.

Unlike the mosquito, the blackfly thrives in running water. Rapidly flowing streams are preferred breeding places. Once able to fly, the female, which feeds by day, is ready for a meal in order to carry out its task of reproduction.

Like the mosquito, the blackfly is found over much of North America, but its largest concentrations are in the woodlands of Canada and the northern reaches of the United States. This insect is abundant throughout late spring and summer, with May and June being the worst months in many areas.

The vicious bite of the blackfly is caused by broad blades found in the mouth parts. These blades make relatively large wounds, which continue to bleed after the fly has fed and gone. The bite often goes unnoticed until a trickle of blood is felt or seen. Blackfly saliva may be toxic, causing pain and itching and sometimes nervous and intestinal disorders.

Not as much is known about the blackfly as about the mosquito, so we can't say what actually draws this insect to its target. But it is thought that the female blackfly detects the carbon dioxide given off by the skin and then follows the convection currents of warm moist air that the host produces.

Repellent Use

Anyone who is going into the backcountry should always carry a good supply of chemical insect repellent, even if the trip is to be a short one. A repellent should always be included in a survival kit. Repellents are the most effective deterrent. They work by confusing the insect and discouraging it from feeding on the victim.

The percentage of DEET in an insect repellent can determine how long the product will give you protection. If the insect repellent you purchase has 10 to 15 percent DEET, you can expect approximately four hours of protection; from 20 to 50 percent, approximately six hours; 50 to 75 percent, approximately eight hours; and 75 to 100 percent, a full day of protection. This varies from person to person, but it is a good rule of thumb to start with.

People who spend a lot of time in the outdoors today are blessed with a number of excellent insect repellents to choose from. I carry BugX repellent single-use towelettes in my survival kit. They take up little space and work well.

When using any of these chemical repellents, you should follow some simple guidelines:

1. Read all label directions carefully.
2. When using aerosol repellents, always keep the spray opening aimed away from your face, and avoid spraying while close to fire.
3. For the best protection, repellent should be applied to all exposed skin except eyes, lips, and open cuts.
4. Avoid repellent contact with outdoor equipment and clothing made of Spandex, rayon, acrylics, or plastics. It can dissolve monofilament fishing line, and plastic lenses in glasses.
5. Reapply repellent after swimming or perspiring heavily, since water or perspiration will weaken a repellent's effectiveness.

Towelettes such as the BugX brand insect repellent, are an excellent way to pack in enough protection to last several days.

Repellents alone will not give you total protection from mosquitoes and blackflies in areas of heavy infestations. A head net may be well worth the bother at certain times.

In bug country, you should always wear a long-sleeved shirt and pants. Apply a repellent containing an appropriate percentage of DEET to the clothing as well as to your exposed skin. To keep the pests from invading the openings of your clothing, use rubber bands or short lengths of cord to tie down your shirt sleeves and pants legs.

When using a repellent, the trick is to apply enough to get complete coverage. According to experts, it takes approximately five seconds of spray time to cover the wrist to the elbow. Most people try to do it in less than one second.

For tick and chigger control, spray clothing and gear, such as day packs, with permethrin. It kills these insects as well as mosquitoes on contact. Be sure to follow the instructions on the label.

In a survival situation during warm weather, pick a campsite with insect control in mind. Stay away from pools of stagnant water. Pick sites that are on high breezy points or at least in the open where you can take advantage of any breeze that may help keep the insects away.

When there is No Repellent

There are often occasions where the lost or stranded person either has run out of repellent or has none and the flying pests are out in vast numbers. When this happens, the first thing to do is to cover up all exposed skin areas. Tuck trouser legs down into boots. Button sleeves tight around the wrist. Pull up shirt and coat collars to protect the neck. Put on a hat and gloves. In short, give the biting critters as small a target as possible.

Next, build a smoky fire near your shelter; at a time like this, the smokier the better. Lie down and put your face near the ground to keep your eyes and nose as free of the smoke as possible. While this may be irritating, it is better than being fed on by flying pests. In severe conditions, build two fires and sit in the middle. There is no good substitute for carrying insect repellent in your survival kit.

TICKS

While ticks are a potential long-term health threat with diseases such as Lyme disease or Rocky Mountain spotted fever, they do not pose the immediate threat that large numbers of flying pests do. Ticks should be avoided, and when found on the body, removed.

The best prevention is to conduct a full-body tick check using a hand-held mirror—your signal mirror may work—to view all parts of your body upon return from tick-infested areas. Look for ticks under the arms, in and around the ears, inside the belly button, behind the knees, between the legs, around the waist, and especially in hair. Examine gear and pets. Ticks can ride into the survival camp on clothing and pets, then attach to a person later, so carefully examine pets, coats, and daypacks.

The recommended way to remove an embedded tick is discussed in Chapter 7, "Survival First Aid."

SPIDERS

Spiders seem to scare almost as many people as snakes do. However, most spiders are harmless to man. In fact, about seven people die from spider bites in North America in any given year. The two North American spiders that can be deadly are the black widow and the brown recluse. (See first aid treatment for these bites in Chapter 7.)

Black Widow Spider

The female black widow is far more of a toxic hazard than the male She has a shiny black body, approximately 0.6 inch long, and usually has a red hourglass-shaped mark on the underside of her globular abdomen On some, the hourglass marking is replaced with several triangles or spots or an irregular longitudinal blotch She has slim black legs with a span of 1.5 inches. The less toxic male is considerably smaller than the female and usually is a patterned brown color.

The black widow spider is slow to bite and prefers no contact with man.

The black widow is found throughout North America except in northern Canada and in Alaska. Most reported human fatalities have occurred in the southeastern states.

The black widow is generally found in its irregular-shaped web near the ground. Common web sites are under stones, loose bark, or water faucets, or in woodpiles, rodent burrows, garages, storage buildings, outhouses, and barns. Most human bites occur when the spider is inadvertently trapped against part of the body or when the web is accidentally touched.

Man is seldom bitten by the black widow, but when it happens, the bite can be serious.

Brown Recluse Spider

The brown recluse is a medium-sized spider with leg span from 0.8 to 1.6 inches and a color range from yellow-tan to dark brown. The most

The brown recluse spider can be identified by the violin-shaped markings on head and thorax.

distinguishing characteristics are its six eyes (most spiders have eight eyes) arranged a semicircle of three pairs on top of the head, and a violin-shaped marking extending from the area of the eyes to the abdomen.

Brown recluse spiders are found throughout much of the United States. They will readily establish populations inside parts of a building that are generally dry, littered, and undisturbed for long periods. The spiders can also be found outside the protected areas under rocks and loose bark. Members of this species are nonaggressive and normally attempt to escape whenever they are threatened. Thus, most instances of bites occur when the spider is inadvertently trapped, such as when the victim puts on clothing in which the spider is hiding, steps barefoot on a wandering spider at night, or cleans storage areas where the spider resides.

Hobo Spider

The hobo spider is found in southern British Columbia, Washington, Oregon, Idaho, western Montana, western Wyoming, and northern Utah.

A hobo spider.

Hobo spiders frequent areas such as log or timber piles, rock piles, holes in logs/trees, or where tall grass meets crevices in soil where they can make their characteristic funnel webs. The webs are funnel shaped, narrow at the bottom, wide at the top. The spider waits in the small hole at the bottom of the funnel for prey to make contact with the web. When it senses a vibration it will emerge from the hole to envenomate its prey.

The hobo spider has a brown front body region where the legs are attached with darker brown markings and brown legs. The abdomen has a distinctive pattern of yellow markings on a gray background, although this pattern can be difficult to discern without the aid of a microscope or hand lens. The pattern is generally more distinctive in immature specimens. Unlike many other similar-looking spiders, hobo spiders do not have dark bands on their legs. Spiders with such banding are not hobo spiders.

Mature female hobo spiders are 3/8 to 5/8-inches long, and male hobo spiders are 9/32 to 9/16 inches in body length. Males have enlarged pedipalps located near the mouth, resembling short legs.

Bites from some other spiders can be painful and can lead to infections, but they do not pose the hazard of toxins associated with the brown recluse, hobo, or black widow.

POTENTIAL DANGERS

Anyone going into wilderness areas should be aware of the potential dangers that exist. I say potential, as many adventurers spend a lifetime of going into the wilderness areas of North America and never encounter any of these threats. Yet every year scores of outings are ruined due to one or more of these dangers occurring, sometimes with fatal consequences. It is better to have thought out these dangers ahead of time and know how to handle them than it is to go on an outing without a clue.

Also, some of these dangers are the reasons some people stay out of the wilderness. Perhaps if they knew more about these dangers and how to avoid them, they would be ready to face the outdoors with a positive attitude and enjoy their outings.

SNAKES

In my survival seminars I can mention that automobile accidents kill some 40,000 Americans each year, and no one becomes troubled. I can tell the students that lightning kills around thirty Americans annually, and no one raises an eyebrow. But the mention of venomous snakes, which kill fewer than a dozen Americans annually, sends everyone squirming or climbing up on chairs. For some unknown reason, snakes scare the otherwise most fearless among us. Basically, this is an excessive fear—a phobia.

Venomous snakes are found in all the states with the exception of Maine, Alaska, and Hawaii. Canada has rattlesnakes in southern British Columbia, Alberta, Saskatchewan, and Ontario. North America's venomous snakes include two species of coral snakes, four subspecies of copperhead, three subspecies of cottonmouth, and sixteen species of rattlesnakes.

Rattlesnakes are known from elevations up to eleven thousand feet in the southern Sierra Nevada of California, to about eight thousand feet on dry, rocky slopes in Montana, and to the tops of the highest mountains in the Appalachians. In spite of this, venomous snakes are rare in high mountains of the West, in northern evergreen forests, and in heavily farmed or urban industrial areas.

A coral snake; note red bands touch yellow bands.

Surprisingly, some species survive well in suburban areas, especially in the southern states. Areas with unusually large populations of venomous snakes include parts of the Great Plains (rattlesnakes), the lower Mississippi Valley and Gulf Coast (rattlesnakes and cottonmouths), and the southern Appalachians (rattlesnakes and copperheads).

Snakebite is by no means rare in the southern and western United States. Incidence is highest in children from five to fifteen years old, and most bites are sustained close to home. Many bites result from deliberate handling of venomous snakes. (Treatment for venomous snakebite is found in Chapter 7.)

Try to learn to identify poisonous snakes and where they are found.

Coral Snake

This pretty but deadly snake is found in the southern United States from the lowlands of North Carolina to the southwestern states. Coral snakes are usually from twenty to thirty inches long. The coral snake has colored rings completely encircling the body. The colors are red, yellow, and black. A positive identification of the coral snake is that the red ring touches the yellow ring. Coral snakes are usually secretive and hide in leaves, logs, stumps, and debris.

The cottonmouth can be aggressive and giving them a lot of space is the best way to deal with them.

Cottonmouth (Water Moccasin)

The color pattern of the cottonmouth, often called water moccasin, is dull and inconspicuous: dark-brown bars on a somewhat lighter background. Many cottonmouths look either dirty brown or uniform black. I have seen some that were difficult to identify because of variance in their color patterns. The most positive identification is the elliptical, cat-like pupil of the eye, but you don't want to be that close in order to identify it. The cottonmouths get their name from their habit of threatening an intruder with open mouth, revealing a cotton-white interior. Although some individual cottonmouths exceed five feet in length, most are from three to four feet long.

The cottonmouth range is much smaller than most people believe. Generally, their range runs south of a line from south-central Texas up through the Mississippi River Basin in Missouri, down along the Tennessee River Basin, and up the East Coast where the elevation is below eight hundred feet. More often than not, supposed cottonmouths turn out to be voracious water snakes that belong to the *Nerodia* species. These snakes are aggressive, and some do resemble the cottonmouth, but they are not venomous.

Though the cottonmouth is much scarcer than many believe, when you encounter one, avoid it. It is curious and is no coward. The cottonmouth is slow to retreat. Many times I have seen one stand its ground when escape would have been easy.

The best prevention against a cottonmouth bite is precaution. When you are in cottonmouth territory, keep your eyes open and always watch where you place your feet and hands. When you travel in a boat, watch overhanging limbs, stumps, logs, and the base of trees. Cottonmouths like to sun themselves, as other snakes do. Several times I have almost grabbed a snake by reaching around a tree to tie up a boat. Look before you put your hands anywhere.

Another place you are likely to encounter a cottonmouth is on the end of your fish stringer. There is no more sobering experience than to pull up a stringer of fish and find a big cottonmouth attached, swallowing one of the fish. That hazard is one reason southern fishermen have an ice chest or live-well in which to keep their catches.

Copperhead

The copperhead's back is pinkish-buff, russet, or orange-brown with dark brown to reddish cross bands; the belly is pinkish-white with large dark spots, or mottling; the top of the head is yellowish to coppery red; the sides are paler; and the end of the tail is yellow in young snakes, black to dark greenish or brown in adults. The cross band is narrow in the center of the back and wide on the sides in eastern

The copperhead is usually slow to anger and well camouflaged for the woodland floor in which he is found.

THE SCOUTING GUIDE TO SURVIVAL

specimens, only slightly narrowed in western ones. The copperhead being a pit viper, the pupil of the eye is elliptical. The average length is two to three feet; maximum, slightly over four feet.

The copperhead is found in the eastern US (Massachusetts to Kansas, south to the Gulf Coast, westward into Trans-Pecos, Texas), and the southern plains. It frequents wooded, hilly country in the North and West, lowlands in the South, and is sometimes plentiful in well-populated areas. Nocturnal in warm weather, it is diurnal in cool weather. In rocky country, it frequently hibernates in rocky dens with rattlesnakes and various nonpoisonous species.

When encountered, the copperhead usually remains coiled and quiet unless closely approached or touched. It vibrates its tail when angry, and often seems reluctant to strike, although some individuals are very irritable.

Copperheads account for the great majority of snakebites received in the eastern United States, exclusive of Florida and the Mississippi Delta. However, fatalities from these bites are almost unknown.

Rattlesnake

Of the poisonous snakes found in North America, the rattlesnake is perhaps the easiest to identify, because of the jointed rattle found at the tip of the tail. However, this is not always the case because the rattle can be broken off. The pupil of the rattlesnake's eye is vertically elliptical, as is that of the copperhead and cottonmouth.

The rattlesnake likes to lay up in the cool shade during the day and venture out to feed at night, a good reason to stay put in your survival camp at night.

The rattlesnake is found throughout the United States except in Maine, Alaska, and Hawaii. It is also found in southern British Columbia, Alberta, Saskatchewan, and Ontario in Canada.

Here are some don'ts to follow when in snake country:

1. Don't put your hands or feet in places you cannot look, and don't put them in places without first looking.
2. Don't turn or lift a rock or fallen tree with your hands. Move it with a stick or with your foot if your ankle and leg are properly protected.
3. Don't disturb snakes.
4. Don't put your sleeping bag near rock piles or rubbish piles or near the entrance to a cave.
5. Don't sit down without first looking around carefully.
6. Don't gather firewood after dark.
7. Don't step over a log if the other side is not visible. Step on it first.
8. Don't enter snake-infested areas without adequate protective clothing.
9. Don't handle freshly killed venomous snakes.
10. Don't crawl under a fence in high grass or in an uncleared area.
11. Don't go out of your way to kill a poisonous snake unless you need the meat to survive. Thousands of people are bitten by snakes each year merely because they try to kill them without knowing anything of their habits or habitats.
12. Don't panic!

Snakes are probably one of the most overrated fears in the outdoors, and the odds are fairly high that you will never see one or, greater yet, get bitten. However, the potential does exist and some commonsense precaution should be taken. Remember, snakes do not want any more contact with you than you with them.

LIGHTNING

Lightning is one of nature's forces that I respect most. I have been the victim of an indirect strike of lightning twice and on numerous occasions I have seen the destruction it can cause in a second.

Here is just one example of how lightning can become a danger within seconds. It was a perfect day as a scoutmaster led his scout troop into the backcountry of the Great Smoky Mountains National Park. Mid-afternoon found the backpackers in a low valley as they walked toward Molly Ridge. Suddenly the bright sky turned dark and a hard rainstorm blew in from behind a tall mountain. Without any warning there was a bright flash and resounding crack as a lightning bolt, the only one of the storm, found its way from the storm cloud to the earth. The lightning forked on its way and hit five trees within a one-hundred-yard diameter. None of the trees were particularly tall as compared to the surrounding trees. From one of the trees, the lightning bolt arced ten feet and struck the scoutmaster's metal pack frame. Traveling down the frame, melting the aluminum as it went, the lightning entered his body at the lower end of the frame where it touches the small of the back. From there it traveled down his legs, shredding his pants into specks of cloth, twisted both ankles and ripped off both boots, and blew off the little toe on the

Lightning is a greater threat than most people realize. The effect of lightning on this tree in New Mexico points up the inadvisability of camping under a tall tree in a lightning storm.

foot that was not touching the ground. Leaving his body, the bolt continued downhill, plowing a ditch as it went. Four other troop members, some one hundred yards away, were knocked down and stunned by the same bolt.

The scoutmaster fell to the ground alive but severely hurt.

The rest of the story is a credit to leadership, training, and courage. Due to the efforts of his scouts and the park rangers, the scoutmaster was in the hospital late that night. It was twenty-six days before he could go home, and he carries the scars today to prove that lightning can be a deadly killer even in low valleys.

Each year in the US lightning, on average, kills thirty people. It is also the greatest single cause of forest fires in the western US, starting over 7,500 fires each year.

Lightning is not only a killer of man, but it also kills many animals each year, both wild and domestic. As I was researching this book, lightning struck a tree in the middle of a pasture near where I live and killed fifty head of beef cattle, weighing about eight hundred pounds each, who were standing under the tree. There are many reports by wildlife biologists each year of deer and elk being killed by lightning.

The coasts of the US over the years have had a high number of lightning fatalities, with a higher-than-average incidence of lightning fatalities and property damage along the Mississippi, Ohio, and Hudson rivers and their drainage basins. The Rocky Mountains are also hard hit by lightning. However, all areas of North America can experience sudden storms with lightning, so the rule for anyone outdoors is to always keep an eye on the weather.

From studies drawn from years of case histories provided by the National Weather Service, the National Climatic Center, and other agencies, it has been possible to draw up a list of useful safety rules for surviving lightning.

First, of course, is to get the latest weather forecast before setting forth to go outside, or before embarking on a recreational outing. If there is a chance of thunderstorm, take a cell phone with a weather app along to get occasional updates, and be ready to seek shelter if a severe thunderstorm watch or warning is announced. The more severe the thunderstorm, the greater the intensity and frequency of lightning strokes.

You don't need an official warning to tell you that a thunderstorm is coming. In almost all cases you can see the towering thunder-head and occasional flashes of lightning at least half an hour in advance. Usually this is ample time to find shelter or take precautions.

When a thunderstorm threatens, all lightning experts agree that the single most important thing you can do is to get inside a home or a large building, or inside an all-metal automobile.

Outdoor recreationists frequently overlook the fact that their automobile is an excellent lightning shelter. This is so because the metal of the car conducts the lightning current around the people safely tucked inside. Many believe the rubber tires insulate the car from a lightning strike. Some of these people also believe it is safe in the bed of a pickup truck or on the seat of a tractor because of the tires, but they are wrong. Lightning, after traveling miles through insulating air, has no trouble flashing across the tires. A car struck by lightning will almost always be found with the occupants unhurt but with the tires blown or aflame.

Other rules to follow:

- Do not stand underneath a natural lightning rod such as a large tree in an open area.
- Avoid projecting above the surrounding landscape, as you would do if you were standing on a hilltop, in an open field, on the beach, paddling a canoe in a lake, or fishing from a small boat.
- Get out of and away from open water. (If you're swimming, lightning current from a nearby stroke can flow through the water to you.)
- Get away from metal objects such as an ATV, barbecue, or wire fence.
- Fishing rods of all materials can become lightning rods if elevated above the hull of a boat or canoe. Lower rods and lay in bottom of craft at the first sight of lightning.
- Avoid standing in small isolated sheds or other small structures in open areas.
- In a forest, seek shelter in a low area under a thick growth of small trees. In open areas, go to a low place such as a ravine or valley.
- Groups of persons in exposed situations, such as hikers or mountain climbers, should spread out—staying several yards apart—so that if lightning strikes nearby, the smallest number will be affected.
- Stay away from water, wet items such as ropes, and metal objects such as fences and poles. Water and metal do not attract lightning but they are excellent conductors of electricity. The current from a lightning flash will easily travel for long distances.

Keeping an eye on the weather and keeping in touch with a current weather report is always the best way to prepare for an electrical storm.

FLASH FLOODING

The transformation of a tranquil river or scenic dry canyon into a destructive flood occurs hundreds of times each year. No area of North America is completely free from the threat of flash flooding.

Take Colorado as an example. Flash floods are no strangers to Colorado outdoorsmen. Since the year 1900, nearly three hundred people have been killed in flash floods across that one state.

In terms of lives lost, the worst flash flood occurred on July 31, 1976 in the Big Thompson Canyon between Estes Park and Loveland, Colorado. A nearly stationary storm produced around twelve inches of rain within four hours, claiming 144 lives, mostly campers.

Flash floods are a fact of life—and death—along the rivers and streambeds and arroyos of North America. They result from rains and/or melting snow filling natural and man-made drainage systems to overflowing with raging water and its deadly cargo of uprooted trees, smashed structures, boulders, mud, and other debris.

The US Department of Commerce's National Oceanic and Atmospheric Administration (NOAA) and its National Weather Service have taken steps to improve the technology and content of our flood warning system and to increase the time available for people to take emergency measures to protect life and property. With flash floods, time is so short and the possibility of tragedy so great that individuals in many areas must also utilize local preparedness plans to help themselves. If you understand the danger of flash flooding and know what immediate action to take, you can save your life.

The National Weather Service has two flash flood alerts which they issue. These alerts should be given everyone's attention in the specific area.

Flash Flood Watch. Heavy rains may result in flash flooding in the specified area. Be alert and prepared for the possibility of a flood emergency that will require immediate action. Have a plan to move to higher ground quickly.

Flash Flood Warning. Flash flooding is occurring or is imminent in the specified areas. Move to safe ground immediately.

Before the flood, know the elevation of your location in relation to nearby streams and other waterways, and make advance plans of what you will do and where you will go in a flash flood emergency.

When a flash flood watch is issued for your area:

- Listen to area radio stations on a battery-operated weather radio or watch weather apps on your cell phone for possible flash flood warnings and reports of flooding in progress from the National Weather Service and public safety agencies.
- Be prepared to move out of danger's way at a moment's notice.
- If you are on a road, watch for flooding at highway dips, bridges, and low areas.
- Watch for signs (thunder, lightning) of distant heavy rainfall. It may not be raining where you are, but it may be pouring down at the upper end of the watershed you are in and a wall of water may be racing toward you.

When a flash flood warning is issued for your area:

- Act quickly to save yourself and those who depend on you. You may have only seconds.
- Do not attempt to cross a flowing stream on foot where water is above your knees. Even then, use a wading pole to keep your balance.
- If you are driving, don't try to ford dips of unknown depth. If your vehicle stalls, abandon it immediately and seek higher ground, as rapidly rising water may sweep the vehicle and its occupants away. Many deaths have been caused by attempts to move stalled vehicles. Remember that it takes little over one foot of water to carry most cars and trucks away. Turn around, don't drown.
- Be especially cautious at night, when it is harder to recognize flood dangers.

After the flash flood watch or warning has been cancelled, stay tuned to radio or weather apps for follow-up information. Flash flooding may have ended, but general flooding may come later in headwater streams and major rivers. Remember, any heavy rain can cause locally destructive flash flooding. Any time you are in the backcountry and it is raining, think flash floods.

Heavy rainfall, even for short periods, may be followed by flash flooding in mountainous or hilly areas. When you go into remote areas, follow these suggestions:

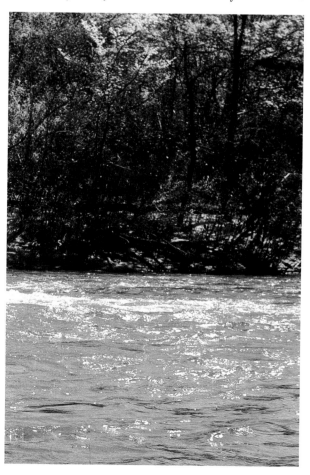

- Stay away from natural streambeds, arroyos, and other drainage channels during and after rainstorms. Water runs off the higher elevations very rapidly.
- Never camp on low ground. A flash flood can catch you while you sleep.
- Use your topo maps. Know where you are and whether you are on low ground.
- Remember, you don't have to be at the bottom of a hill to be a target for flash flood dangers.
- Know where the high ground is and how to get there.
- Stay out of flooded areas.
- Keep alert to signs of wet weather, either rain where you are or signs of rain, including thunder and nearby lightning.
- Keep as informed as you can.

If you are out of range of broadcast/cell phone information, be sure to watch for these indicators of flash flooding:

- Storms nearby.
- Increase in the speed of river flow.
- Rapid rise in river level.

Be prepared to move to safety quickly.

FALLS

Falls are one of the most common accidents that happen in the wilderness each year. An attractive waterfall, cliff, log over a rushing stream, muddy slope, or cave can all be the attraction that can cause a serious fall and resulting injuries that lead to a stranding and a survival situation. People who become lost often panic and start running, and that can lead to serious falls. Falls and the resulting injuries or death are one of the most frequent reasons for search and rescue efforts.

A book could be written about how to prevent falls in the wilderness, but here are just a few of the precautions to take:

- Falls can result in serious injuries or death and put you in a survival situation fast. Take fall prevention seriously. Don't take chances.
- Watch where you are walking. Wet leaves, tree roots, mud, ice, snow, wet grass, and wet logs have all led to serious injuries of even experienced backcountry travelers.
- When walking near the edges of bluffs or cliffs, watch for loose or crumbling rocks. Resist the temptation to go to the edge. Keep a safe distance from edges.
- Hurrying puts you at risk of falling. Slow down and enjoy the outing.
- Wear proper footwear, with soles to match the terrain.
- Use a bright light at night.

There are a lot more emergency calls made in the backcountry for fall victims each year than for snakebites, spider bites, and bear attacks combined. Use common sense as to where to climb or put your feet when on an outing.

BEAR ATTACK

One of the most common fears of inexperienced wilderness travelers is an attack from a bear. From time to time, people are indeed attacked by bears, both grizzly and black bears. In most cases, this is the fault of the people, not the bears, because bears don't normally hunt people. The most dangerous bears are those that have become accustomed to people, especially in parks, campgrounds, and garbage dumps. These bears have lost their fear of man and can be highly unpredictable.

Basically, bears like to keep their distance from humans, but when human and bear are suddenly thrown together, the result can be grim for the human. Anyone who accidentally gets between a grizzly sow and her cubs is in serious trouble, for example.

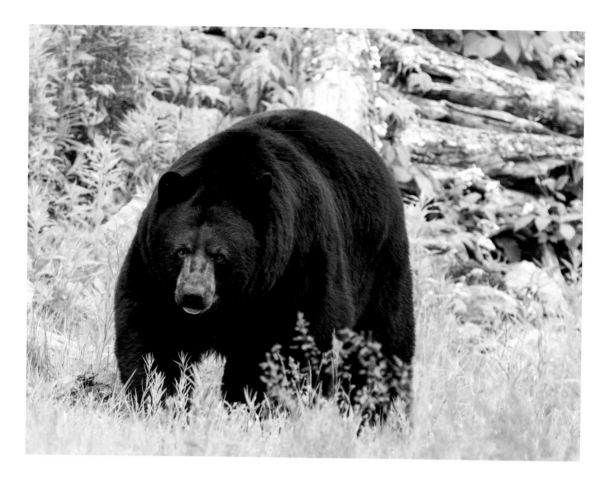

Bears shouldn't keep you from enjoying the outdoors, but when you are going into bear country, you should know what to do and what not to do in order to live in harmony with these powerful animals.

If planning a trip into bear country, obtain information about the area and if bears are found in the area. Much of the US is free of bears, so in these areas the bear threat is nonexistent. However, if bears are living in the area that you plan on traveling through, then a few precautions can keep you out of trouble.

Be Prepared for a Bear Encounter

If going into bear country, include a can of bear spray in your equipment and keep it where you can get to it quickly in the unlikely event it should be needed. Always select an EPA-approved product that is specifically designed to stop bears. Personal defense, jogger defense, law enforcement or military defense sprays may not contain the correct ingredients, or have the proper delivery system, to stop a charging bear.

Only use bear spray products that clearly state "for deterring attacks by bears." EPA-registered bear sprays have an active ingredient, clearly shown on the label, of 1 to 2 percent capsaicin and related capsaicinoids (found in chili peppers). This active ingredient is what affects the bear's eyes, nose, mouth, throat, and lungs.

EPA-registered bear sprays have a minimum duration of at least six seconds to compensate for multiple bears; wind; bears that may zigzag, circle, or charge multiple times; and for the hike out after you have stopped a charging bear.

EPA-registered bear sprays shoot a minimum distance of twenty-five feet, a distance at which the active ingredients will reach the bear at sufficient strength to affect it in time to divert or stop the bear's charge and give it time to retreat.

Bear spray is intended to be sprayed into the face of an oncoming bear. Factors influencing effectiveness include distance, wind, rainy weather, temperature extremes, and product shelf life. It is not intended to act as a repellent. Do not spray gear or your camp with bear spray. Pre-sprayed objects may actually attract bears.

Visitors in bear country should carry a can of bear spray in an easily accessible fashion. Bear spray should also be readily available in the sleeping, cooking, and toilet areas of backcountry camps.

It's important to be sure the expiration date on your bear spray is current. It's equally important to study how to use it in advance and to follow the manufacturer's instructions. Know how to use the spray, and be aware of its limitations.

Leave the safety clip on the trigger unless you are ready to spray an aggressive bear. The spray may accidentally discharge otherwise. If you use the spray to stop a bear, leave the area immediately.

Under no circumstances should bear spray create a false sense of security or serve as a substitute for standard safety precautions in bear county.

If You Surprise a Bear in the Wild

Stand still, stay calm, and let the bear identify you and leave. Talk in a normal tone of voice. Be sure the bear has an escape route.

Never run or climb a tree.

If you see cubs, their mother is usually close by. Leave the area immediately.

If the Bear Doesn't Leave

A bear standing up is just trying to identify what you are by getting a better look and smell.

Wave your arms slowly overhead and talk calmly. If the bear huffs, pops its jaws, or stomps a paw, it wants you to give it space.

If on a trail, step off the trail to the downhill side, keep looking at the bear, and slowly back away until the bear is out of sight.

If the Bear Approaches

A bear knowingly approaching a person could be a food-conditioned bear looking for a handout or, very rarely, an aggressive bear. Stand your ground. Yell or throw small rocks in the direction of the bear. Don't feed him!

Get out your bear spray and use it when the bear is about forty feet away. Try to spray downwind, not upwind, so the spray doesn't blow back and get you.

If you're attacked, don't play dead. Fight back with anything available. People have successfully defended themselves with knives, hiking sticks, and even bare hands.

Keeping Bears Out of Camp

National Parks are likely to offer storage lockers or food poles at campsites; wilderness campsites will often require you to find your own tree suitable for hanging your food from. Bring at least thirty feet of rope or paracord and enough stuff sacks to hang your food, garbage, and scented items from food poles or trees. Plan on bringing at least one stuff sack for every two people in your group. Waterproof stuff sacks are best in case it rains. You can also seal everything inside your stuff sack into a smell-proof plastic bag to keep both the contents dry and the smells more contained.

Pick a tree that is at least one hundred yards from your survival camp. Hang your food sacks from a branch that is at least ten feet off the ground, with the sack hanging at least four feet from the trunk of the tree.

Bears will usually move out of the way if they hear people approaching, so make noise. Don't surprise bears! Bear bells are often not sufficient. Calling out (try saying "Hey Bear") and clapping your hands at regular intervals are better ways to make your presence known.

Some trail conditions make it hard for bears to hear, see, or smell approaching hikers. Be particularly careful near streams, when it's windy, in dense vegetation, or in any circumstance that limits line of sight (e.g. a blind corner or rise in the trail).

Never intentionally get close to a bear. Individual bears have their own personal space requirements that vary depending on their mood. Each bear will react differently, and a bear's behavior cannot be predicted. All bears are wild and dangerous and should be respected equally.

MOUNTAIN LION ATTACK

Mountain lions, sometimes called pumas or cougars, are making a comeback in many areas, but much of the US and Canada is free of mountain lions. As with bears, check to see if mountain lions are present in the area before you go on a backcountry outing. Even if they are, the chances of seeing one are very slim, and if you do, consider yourself special, as they are magnificent animals.

Should you encounter a mountain lion, here is what the Mountain Lion Foundation (www.mountainlion.org) recommends you should do:

- Stay back and take the encounter seriously.
- Seem as large as possible. Make yourself appear larger. Open your jacket, raise your arms slowly.
- Make noise, yell, shout, bang your walking stick or water bottle. Make any loud sound that cannot be confused by the lion as the sound of prey. Speak slowly and loudly to disrupt and discourage the lion's hunting instincts.
- Act defiant, not afraid. Maintain eye contact. Never run past or away from a mountain lion.
- Don't bend over or crouch down. Aggressively wave your arms, throw stones or branches, do not turn away.
- Slowly create distance. Assess the situation. Consider whether you may be between the lion and its kittens, prey, or cache. Back away slowly to give the mountain lion a path to retreat, never turning your back.
- Give the lion the time and ability to get away.

SURVIVE A VEHICLE STRANDING

Perhaps one of the most common strandings in North America is the broken-down automobile, truck, or SUV. We see them alongside our roads and highways every day. For the people involved, the stranding is usually nothing more a nuisance, as help is nearby. However, for those people who travel into little-traveled areas, such as national forest roads, and suddenly find themselves stranded, the situation can become serious quickly.

Anyone going anywhere with a vehicle—car, truck, ATV, trail bike, or snowmobile—should let someone know their plans. This is especially true if the trip, long or short, takes the vehicle off the beaten path. File a trip plan. Where are you going, when do you plan to arrive at your destination, when do you plan to return? If you should turn up missing, the authorities would have something to go on.

Always keep your vehicle in good working order by having it checked before trips. Fan belts account for many stranded situations each year, as does running out of fuel. Make sure your belts are in good shape and carry a spare with tools. Plan the fuel for your trips on the one-third tank rule: one-third tank going, one-third tank returning, and one-third tank in reserve.

If it is doubtful that your vehicle can make a trip, don't take it.

Watch the weather. Each winter we read of people who get caught in snow and ice storms and are found dead by rescue teams. Our need to go gets many of us in trouble every winter.

Listen to a weather report applicable for the area you will be traveling in before you depart on a trip. If the weather service reports storm warnings, stay home. If you get caught in a snow storm, stay with your vehicle. Have survival gear and rest up for rescue. If possible, keep the top of the vehicle free of snow so that it can be seen from the air. Carry a bright orange panel if your car color blends in with the snow.

CARRY SURVIVAL GEAR

Every vehicle should carry basic survival gear that is upgraded periodically to match the season and the terrain in which you will be traveling. A fully equipped survival kit should be carried. A

Even an ATV can get hopelessly stuck, resulting in the rider being stranded in a remote area.

well-charged cell phone should always be in any vehicle that doesn't have an on-board communications device.

Another vital survival item that all vehicles should carry is a portable air compressor. This handy device takes care of low tires on passenger vehicles, 4X4 vehicles, pickups, RVs, motorcycles, ATVs, and bicycles on the spot. It plugs into a vehicle's twelve-volt socket and usually has a long power cord and three-foot air hose. Some models are run on rechargeable batteries. There is a positive latching tire valve connector with pressure check stem to allow pressure checking without removing the connector from the tire. The air compressor fits compactly in the vehicle trunk or storage area.

Additional survival items that you should keep in your vehicle include a first aid kit, one gallon of water (much more if you are traveling in desert country), emergency food, matches in a waterproof container, basic tools for repairs, spare parts, tow rope, rain gear, shovel, ax, and, during cold weather, tire chains and one sleeping bag per person.

During cool or cold weather, your vehicle makes an excellent shelter and is easy to spot, so there is no need to leave it. Since most cars are tightly built, keep a window slightly open to allow oxygen to enter. This is especially true if you are burning anything in the car or running the motor to keep warm.

In extremely hot weather, the vehicle can become an oven. Seek shelter in the shade around or under the vehicle.

FOUR-WHEEL-DRIVE VEHICLES

My work in wildlife management brings me into contact each year with hundreds of sportsmen who are using four-wheel-drive vehicles to get into the backcountry. Many of these people are experienced outdoorsmen but are somewhat inexperienced in driving through mud, large rocks, and sand. I see scores of these vehicles stuck, and most could have avoided the problem.

A lot of new owners of four-wheelers, and there are thousands every year now, think just because they paid $60,000 for their vehicle and it has big tires, plus a winch, that it can swim through the deepest mud hole or fly over the largest rock pile. This attitude can only lead to trouble.

Let's start from the beginning and see how the driver of a four-wheel-drive vehicle should approach backcountry driving.

Get your vehicle ready for the trip. Proper tires should have round shoulders and a moderately aggressive tread such as the standard mud-grip or all-weather tread. You should have a power winch installed if your budget can stand the cost. You should also have a tool chest that includes snow chains (even though you don't expect snow), shovel, ax, compact air compressor, two jacks, fifty-foot nylon rope for towing (10,000-pound test), two two-inch-thick by one-foot-wide by two-foot-long planks, and a set of wrenches.

If you don't have a winch, be sure and add what's known as a "come-along" to your tool chest. The come-along is simply a hand-powered winch. It is best described as a hand-cranked, cable-filled wheel and ratchet. You attach one end of the cable to a tree and the come-along to the vehicle frame. Each time you pump the handle, the wheel takes up the cable, winching you out of the mud hole.

Once you leave maintained roads, the trick is to travel slowly and study the road carefully. If there is any doubt about the condition of the road ahead, stop, get out of your vehicle, and do a little walking. How deep is the mud, or how deep is the hole under the water? Use a stick and test each situation. Common sense should tell you when to turn around and find a new route.

If the going looks as though it's going to get rough, put on your tire chains. They work as well in slick mud as they do in snow. Another trick to use, especially in deep sand, is to decrease your tire pressure to approximately twelve pounds. This allows your tires to "float." Don't forget to inflate them again as you get out of the trouble area.

Learn to use your winch (or your come-along) before you actually need it. Numerous times I have come upon a shiny new four-wheel-drive vehicle stuck and found that the owner did not know how to use his winch. When you buy your winch, make sure the salesman gives you a good session in its proper and safe use.

The most frustrating situation, and one of the most common emergencies that four-wheelers find themselves in, is to have all four wheels stuck, unable to move forward or backward. If you have an electric winch, the solution is to hook the cable to a tree and throw the switch. If you don't have a winch, then hook up your come-along and be prepared to sweat a little. Use your shovel to clear the way for each tire to move. If you don't have either of these devices, a third possibility is to get an accompanying vehicle to pull you out.

If you have none of these options, you are in for some work. You must shovel away all the mud that's piled up underneath the vehicle. This is supporting the weight of the chassis and keeping weight off the tires, thereby causing the tires to lose traction.

Once you have the vehicle's under-carriage free of mud, get out a jack and plank. Using the plank as a platform for the jack, raise the wheel that is deepest in the mud. Dig out the mud beneath the wheel down to a firm base. Then fill up the hole with rocks, logs, brush, and such. Now lower the wheel slowly down onto the firm platform you've constructed. Do the same thing to each of the other wheels. Then extend the solid platforms for several feet in front of each wheel. If you don't, you'll be able to move forward only a few feet and then will be back into the same predicament.

Sandy areas should be traveled over with caution. The important thing to remember in sand or soft dirt is to keep moving steadily and not too fast. Don't apply an excess of power that would cause the wheels to dig in. Try to avoid abrupt changes in speed or direction, and aim as straight as possible across the area. Avoid sharp turns, as sharp turns cause the front tires to scrub sideways, turning them into plows that can raise impassable pileups of the sand. It would take a book to list the various ways people get stuck in the backcountry with their vehicles and the ways to get them out. If only they would learn the capabilities and limits of their vehicles and how to read backcountry roads, most of these situations would be avoided. Unavoidable pitfalls can be remedied in a short time by knowing how to use your emergency equipment and applying it with a little common sense.

THE VEHICLE AS A SURVIVAL TOOL

The vehicle can aid your survival in many ways. The mirrors can be used for signaling. The battery can produce sparks for fire starting. The cigarette lighter can start proper burning for fire starting. Hubcaps can be used for shovels or buckets or cooking vessels. Floor mats can be used to give wheels traction to get unstuck. The spare tire can be used as a seat to get you up off hot sand or burned for a smoke signal. Wiring from a car can be used for snares. The list could go on and on.

The vehicle can provide you with a vast variety of survival tools, but if you carry the proper survival gear this will not have to be necessary.

IF A BLIZZARD TRAPS YOU IN YOUR CAR

If you get caught in a snow storm, stay with your vehicle. Have survival gear and rest up for rescue. If possible, keep the top of the vehicle free of snow so that it can be seen from the air. Carry a bright orange panel if your car color blends in with the snow. Here are some rules to follow:

- Stay in the vehicle. Do not attempt to walk in a blizzard. Disorientation comes quickly in blowing and drifting snow. Being lost in open country during a blizzard is extremely dangerous. You are more likely to be found in your car and will at least be sheltered there.
- Avoid overexertion and exposure. Exertions from attempting to push your car, shoveling heavy drifts, and performing other difficult chores during strong winds, blinding snow, and bitter cold of a blizzard may cause a heart attack—even for persons in apparently good physical condition.
- Keep a downwind window slightly open for fresh air. Freezing rain, wet snow, and wind-driven snow can completely seal the passenger compartment.
- Beware of carbon monoxide. Run the engine, heater, or catalytic heater sparingly, and only with a downwind window open for ventilation. Make sure that snow has not blocked the exhaust pipe.
- Exercise by clapping your hands and moving your arms and legs vigorously from time to time, and do not stay in one position for long. But don't overdo it. Exercise warms you, but it also increases body heat loss.
- If more than one person is in the vehicle, don't sleep at the same time. Take turns keeping watch for searchers.
- Turn on the dome light occasionally at night to make sure your vehicle is more visible to working or search crews.
- Don't panic. Stay with the car.

17

DOWNED AIRCRAFT SURVIVAL

"Mayday, Mayday, Mayday." This emergency code comes in from many airplanes in trouble. In fact, the Civil Air Patrol participates an average of one thousand search missions each year, most of which are for downed aircraft. Most of the people in these aircraft never thought it would happen to them. One minute they were comfortably flying over rough, remote terrain, the next minute they were on the ground in a survival situation.

According to the Civil Air Patrol, of every one hundred persons involved in air crashes, only thirty-five will survive initially, only eighteen will survive for twenty-four hours, and fewer than ten will live more than seventy-two hours.

Some of the after-crash deaths can be avoided. With the proper survival gear, survival training, and a will to live, many of these people could live for days or weeks.

WHAT TO DO BEFORE YOU FLY
Before anyone, either passenger or pilot, takes off on a private plane trip, he should make sure that a few basic rules are followed.

File a flight plan
Be sure a flight plan is filed, and stay with the plan. If you change your plans while flying, notify the Federal Aviation Administration (FAA) of this change at once. Upon arrival at your destination, file an arrival report. Remember that a search normally starts after you fail to report in and enough time has passed that your fuel is exhausted—usually about three hours. Don't delay the arrival report.

When no flight plan is filed, the rescue attempt can be delayed for a long time or may never happen.

Check the Emergency Locator Transmitter
The Emergency Locator Transmitter (ELT), usually located in the tail of the aircraft, has proven to be the best aid to searchers and the best hope for timely rescue of survivors of air crashes.

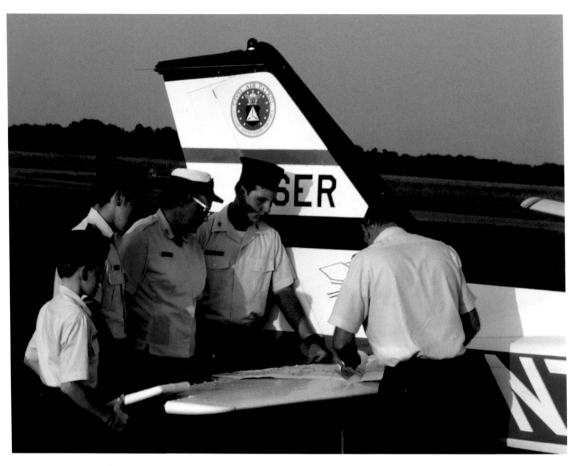

Once an aircraft is reported missing, the Civil Air Patrol jumps into action and a logical search is begun immediately.

The ELT is a small electronic box which can beam out a strong signal when activated. It is activated upon the plane's impact with the ground. This signal can be picked up by commercial and military aircraft. It can also be picked up by satellites that are carrying a SARSAT (Search and Rescue Satellite Aided Tracking) package. With the aid of the SARSAT satellites, the science of finding aircraft and oceangoing vessels in distress has taken a giant step. Don't fly in a plane that doesn't have an ELT.

Carry Survival Gear

Be sure your plane has a survival kit and survival gear. The survival gear should be stored in a daypack so that it will be kept together in the plane, making it easy to retrieve after a crash and easy to carry if you must change locations. Don't forget to include food and water in your survival gear. You could be in for a long wait.

Dress and Equip Yourself According to Ground Weather

It is important for you to dress according to the ground weather you will be flying over. You may choose to dress in light clothing because you may be going from warm airport to warm plane to warm airport. However, if you're forced down in cold mountains along the way, you don't have much of a chance of survival. If you don't want to wear the clothing, at least take it with you. A sleeping bag per person should be taken during cold weather. Rain gear should be taken during wet weather.

Watch the weather along the entire route and cancel or postpone the trip if there is any question concerning the weather or changes in weather. If your route takes you over large bodies of water, take along a self-inflatable life raft and know how to use it.

When You Go Down

Here are steps to take if your aircraft goes down:

1. Get the survival gear and exit the aircraft immediately (thus the reason to have it packed in a day pack).
2. Move everyone a safe distance from the aircraft to avoid dangers from fire and explosions. Wait until the engines have cooled and spilled aviation fuel has evaporated before returning to the aircraft.
3. Treat the injured as quickly as possible.
4. While awaiting your return to the aircraft, make temporary shelter to protect everyone from inclement weather.
5. Get signals ready for use in the event searchers reach the area quickly.
6. Reassure everyone, including yourself, and remain calm.
7. If the aircraft radios are still serviceable, they should momentarily be tuned to the distress frequency to ensure that the ELT is operating. Once the ELT is activated, it must be left on, since turning it off can result in a search aircraft being thwarted in its attempt to home in on the transmission.
8. If the aircraft radios are operational, try to make contact with the FAA on a local frequency.
9. Search the aircraft for items that you may have to use in survival—maps, clothing, tools.
10. At this point, a major decision must be reached, and that is whether to stay with the aircraft or leave the crash site. The basic rule is to stay with the aircraft if at all possible, since searchers will be looking for it soon and because it has an ELT working for you. You will also avoid the possible hazards of travel. Your chances will be good if you have made radio contact; if you have come down on course or near a traveled air route; or if weather and air observation conditions are good.
11. The aircraft is generally easier to spot from the air than by people traveling on foot. Someone may even have seen your plane go down and may be along to investigate. The aircraft or parts from it can provide you with shelter, signaling aids, and other equipment. If the temperature is neither too cold nor too hot, the cabin of the plane can be used a shelter. However, in temperature extremes, the cabin can be an oven or refrigerator. If the weather is cold, the plane's insulation and upholstery can be used to make items such as sleeping

If your aircraft is downed, gather anything that you think you may need for survival purposes.

bags, caps, or mattresses. Wings, rudders, or doors may be used to make shelter. The battery can provide a spark for fire-starting. Such items as maps, curtains, and newspapers can be used to improve the shelter and to provide warmth. Use cowling for reflector signals, tubing for shelter framework, and the generator for radio power.

There are rare occasions, however, when you may need to move some distance from the aircraft, such as if it is down under trees and cannot be seen from the air, as in the classic case of Helen Klaben and Ralph Flores. The pair left Whitehorse, Yukon, heading for San Francisco in a small private airplane, neither had survival training. Over the Yukon-British Columbia border, they ran into a blinding snowstorm which caused them to crash.

For over a month, search and rescue aircraft flew over the area looking for the downed plane, but the thick trees in which Helen and Ralph had crashed hid the plane from view.

Both Helen and Ralph were injured in the crash, but they managed to set up a survival camp at the aircraft. They had very little survival gear on the plane: matches, a little food, some vitamin pills, two tubes of toothpaste, a hammer, cold chisel, hunting knife, books, canvas motor cover, and extra clothing. For a blanket, they tore the carpet from the plane floor and insulation from

Stay with the downed aircraft if it is safe to do so, as this is where the searchers will be looking.

the walls and ceiling. Seat and back cushions were used for beds. Firewood was cut with the chisel and hammer. During their ordeal, temperatures dropped to -40 F.

Their food ran out the first week. From then on, it was only water, which they got by melting snow in a can. Their drinking cup was made from a light reflector from the plane. They made several attempts to kill rabbits that came near their camp, but nothing worked.

For thirty-three days they stayed with the aircraft, but after hearing forty to fifty aircraft pass nearby, they decided they must move if they were to be found. On snowshoes made from branches and a toboggan made from aircraft parts, they moved their meager supplies through deep snow to an opening in the forest. Since they were very weak, this three-quarters-of-a-mile journey was quite tough. Here they used the engine cover tarpaulin to make a tent. Ralph then moved to another clearing about two miles distant and tramped SOS in the snow, as well as an arrow aimed in Helen's direction. Also, they placed in the snow a fragment of their plane which showed the plane's identification number.

This new camp and signals resulted in their being found. A bush pilot flying supplies to trappers spotted the SOS and the arrow, and then Helen and Ralph. They were rescued forty-nine days after crashing into the frozen wilderness.

If your aircraft is hidden, the first thing to do is try to cut trees and brush to make it visible from the air. If this is impossible, move only a short distance to the first clearing you can find, and set up your ground-to-air sign.

Organize for Rescue

If you are with a group of survivors, organize them and your camp so that everyone who is able will stay busy and the camp will be prepared for comfort until rescue arrives.

The first step in organizing is to appoint individual members to specific jobs, based on their abilities and their physical and mental capacities to handle them. With one person in charge, pool all food and equipment. Prepare a shelter to protect everyone from rain, sand, snow, wind, cold, or insects. Collect all possible firewood, the variety of which will be determined by your geographical location. Always try to have at least one day's supply of wood on hand. Then look for water. Make sure your signals are always in good shape and ready for instant use.

Reassure everyone, and try to keep the will to live alive even if rescue is several days in coming. As we saw in the beginning of this chapter, many survivors of aircraft crashes die while waiting for rescue. This is an unnecessary loss of life. By carrying the necessary survival gear, taking precautions such as filing flight plans, learning survival techniques, and using survival skills when the aircraft is down, you should make it through aircraft survival situations.

At no time attempt to move unless you know exactly where you are and where you are going. To wander aimlessly uses up vital energy that is very difficult to replace under survival conditions. If you are leaving a crash site, even for a short distance, leave a message for rescuers indicating the date and direction of your travel. Regardless of your reason for moving, consider the weather. Stay put if adverse weather would further endanger you. If travel for help is indicated, send the most fit people—two, if possible. To travel alone is dangerous.

Make a definite plan to follow. Determine the nearest rescue point, the distance to it, the possible difficulties and hazards of travel, and the facilities and supplies at the destination. Travel is extremely risky unless you have the necessities of survival to support you during travel. You should have sufficient water to reach the next possible source of water as indicated on your map or chart, enough food to last until you are able to procure additional food, and a means of shelter.

While this chapter has given some pointers on traveling away from the crash site, such travel is not usually recommended. The most important rule of downed aircraft survival is to stay with the aircraft.

1X

SURVIVING VARIOUS ENVIRONMENTS

Hiking, backpacking, wilderness exploring, conservation projects, fishing, hunting, canoeing, and a vast number of other outings can carry a person into environments that are different than what they are accustomed to or are totally foreign to them. Each of these environments has its own weather patterns, terrain, vegetated cover, and challenges. Survival in each of these environments increases with the knowledge of the environment and how well the outing is planned using this knowledge.

WOODLANDS

Across North America there are a wide variety of woodlands ranging from wet rainforest to semi-arid brush country. Most people think of woodlands as park-like places containing a wealth of survival materials for making shelter, fire, signals, and finding water. While in some cases that is true, that may not be the case in others or in severe weather conditions. A rainstorm can make everything wet and difficult to use. Some rainforests are that way most of the time.

Heavy woodlands can have a thick canopy, making signaling to aircraft almost impossible and their seeing you very difficult. Finding an opening may be difficult or you may have to create one. A heavily canopied woodland is one place a signal fire is most valuable, as thick smoke may find its way to the top of the canopy, where searchers can see it. Care must be taken with the fire, as you don't want to start a forest fire. You have enough problems without that.

Damp woodlands can be cold even in the deep South. Some woodlands get heavy snow, which can make travel almost impossible and survival become a race to stay warm and dry.

In a semi-arid forest, finding water can be near impossible, while forest where there is plenty of water may be swarming with mosquitoes or blackflies by the millions, depending on the season. Be prepared.

In flat woodlands, keeping a sense of direction can be nearly impossible without navigational aids. On a cloudy day, woodlands of this type are the easiest to get lost in, even near home.

Here are some tips to consider when planning a trip into woodlands:

- Study the woodlands you plan on going into. Get to know the woods for the season and weather when you plan your outing.
- Study topo maps of the woods and plan your trip carefully. Take the map, compass, and GPS with you.
- File a trip plan.
- Get a weather forecast for the period you plan on being in the woods.
- Dress for the weather and the conditions you anticipate. Carry clothing for unexpected weather such as rain or a drop in temperature. Wear correct boots for the conditions.
- Carry insect repellent in your survival kit, plus extra repellent if the area is known for mosquitoes or blackflies.
- Use navigational aids from the very beginning of the trip. To get lost in a vast, flat hardwood bottom is the wrong time to break out the map and compass.

MOUNTAINS

The mountain environment, whether it is in the southern Appalachians of Georgia or the Brooks Range of Alaska, can be one of sudden weather changes. In the Cassiar Mountains of British Columbia, within one hour I have seen warm sunshine, rain, sleet, and heavy snow. In the Snowbird Mountains of North Carolina, I have seen weather go from a bright, bluebird day to a fierce electrical storm with little advance warning.

Mountain Dangers

The basic rule of mountain survival is to understand the dangers of the mountains, put a lot of planning into any trip into the mountains, and go prepared. If a survival crisis should occur in the mountains, travel should be halted as soon as is practical. Rarely can you improve your lot by trying to struggle out of the mountains. It is usually wiser to establish a position where you can be easily seen and then await rescue.

Falls

Falls and the survival situations resulting from falls probably account for more search and rescue efforts in the mountain environment than any other hazard. These mishaps can occur not only to those involved in the seemingly more dangerous mountain sports, such as mountain climbing, rappelling, and other rock-climbing activities, but to anyone exploring, hiking, fishing, or hunting in a mountainous terrain. Even a relaxing afternoon of fly fishing in a beautiful mountain stream can become deadly if a sudden fall breaks a hip.

A fall in the mountains is a life-threatening occurrence. You cannot be too careful to avoid this very real and ever-present danger.

Lightning

The fiercest electrical storm I have ever witnessed occurred the first year that I guided in Colorado. I had a pack string of animals above timberline one afternoon when, without warning, an electrical storm hit. Lightning was popping the rocks along the mountaintop on which we were riding. The horses were going crazy, and there was little for us riders to do but get off, go down the side of the mountain, spread out, and lie flat on the ground. The storm lasted for almost an hour. It was one of the most frightening hours I have ever spent.

Electrical storms are to be expected in mountains during the warm months, accompanied by large hail. You must keep a constant eye on the weather and make an effort to drop below timberline or get out from under high trees when an electrical storm is approaching. Although thunderstorms are local in nature and usually short in duration, they can be a real threat.

Wind

In high mountains, the ridges and passes are seldom calm. But in protected alleys, strong winds are rare. Normally, wind velocity increases with altitude, since the earth's frictional drag is strongest near the ground, and this effect is accentuated by mountainous terrain. Winds are accelerated when they are forced over ridges and peaks or when they converge through mountain passes and canyons. Because of these funneling effects, the winds may blast with greater force on an exposed mountainside or summit. In most cases, the local wind direction is controlled by topography.

The force exerted by wind quadruples each time the wind speed doubles; that is, wind blowing at 40 miles per hour pushes four times harder than does wind blowing 20 miles per hour. At increasing wind strengths, gusts become more important and may be 50 percent higher than average wind velocity. Always have a place to seek shelter if the wind speed increases.

Dehydration

High mountain air is dry, especially in winter when the humidity in the air condenses into ice. This dryness increases with the altitude. The amount of vapor in the air decreases in geometric proportion as the altitude increases. Consequently, dehydration is a common problem with people in the mountains. Drink water, even if you aren't thirsty, to avoid this condition.

Flash Floods

Since many mountains receive heavy rainfall, particularly near the top, flash flooding is common. It is not unusual for a pleasant brook to suddenly become a rushing wall of water. When camping, keep flash floods in mind. Especially when you are under the stress of a survival situation, avoid setting up your camp close to a creek, low drainage depression, or in a dry wash, as you may be placing yourself in the path of a flash flood.

Snow

Snow can cause many problems for winter mountain travelers, including hampered travel. Many times each fall, news reports from Rocky Mountain states announce that hunters are snowed in and that rescue efforts are under way.

Associated with snow slopes is the avalanche. Even small avalanches can have tremendous force and are a serious threat. Snow avalanches are complex natural phenomena. Since experts do not fully understand all the causes, it is difficult to predict avalanche conditions with certainty.

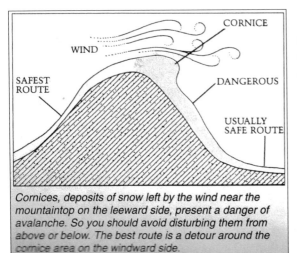

Cornices, deposits of snow left by the wind near the mountaintop on the leeward side, present a danger of avalanche. So you should avoid disturbing them from above or below. The best route is a detour around the cornice area on the windward side.

The more time you spend in high country skiing, snowshoeing, snowmobiling, and engaged in other winter activities, the greater are your chances of being caught by an avalanche.

Survival in Avalanche Areas

The safest routes are on ridgetops and slightly on the windward side away from cornices. Windward slopes are usually safer than leeward slopes. If you cannot travel on ridges, the next safest route is out in the valley, far from the bottom of slopes subject to descent of avalanches.

Avoid disturbing cornices from below or above. Gain ridgetops by detouring around cornice areas.

If you must cross dangerous slopes, stay high and near the top. If you see avalanche fracture lines in the snow, avoid them and similar snow areas.

If you must ascend or descend a dangerous slope, go straight up or down; do not make traverses back and forth across the slope.

Take advantage of areas of dense timber, ridges, or rocky outcrops as islands of safety. Use them for lunch and rest stops. Spend as little time as possible on open slopes.

Snowmobiles should not cross the lower part of the slopes. Do not drive a snowmobile across especially long, open slopes or known avalanche paths.

Obey posted signs put up by authorities, closing slopes because of danger. If you must cross a dangerous slope, only one person at a time should cross. All others should watch. To cross a dangerous slope, remove ski pole straps and ski safety straps, loosen all equipment, put on mitts and cap, and fasten clothing before you travel.

Authorities now recommend that all members of a party in avalanche country carry transceivers, which are pocket-size devices that can transmit and receive signals. When crossing avalanche-prone terrain, all members of the party switch into the transmit mode. Then, if one or more members are caught and buried, other members switch into the receive mode and home in on the victims. Probe poles that can be assembled in sections are also highly useful in probing for victims.

If you are caught in an avalanche:

- Discard all equipment.
- Get away from your snowmobile.
- Make swimming motions. Try to stay on top; work your way to the side of the avalanche.
- Before coming to a stop, get your hands in front of your face and try to make an air space in the snow.
- Try to remain calm.

If you are the survivor:

- Mark the place where you last saw victims.
- Search for victims directly downslope below the last seen point; if they are not on the surface, probe the snow with a pole or stick.
- Do not desert victims and go for help, unless help is only a few minutes away.

Remember, you must consider not only the time required for you to get help, but the time required for help to return. After thirty minutes, the buried victim has only a 50 percent chance of surviving.

If there is more than one survivor:

- Send one for help while the others search for the victim.
- Have the one who goes for help switch his transceiver to transmit mode, in case he gets buried by another avalanche. He should also mark the route effectively so a rescue party can follow back.
- Contact the ski patrol, local sheriff, or Forest Service.
- Administer first aid.
- Treat for suffocation and shock.

For information on the existence of possible avalanche conditions in an area, check the local weather forecasts and contact the Forest Service snow ranger or the nearest winter sports area ski patrol.

Mountain Trip Planning

Anytime you are going into the mountains, the trip should be planned carefully. The route taken, the condition of the roads to and from the mountains, the short-range and long-range weather forecast, and all other aspects of the trip should be carefully researched.

If it is an outing in bear country, check ahead to see if there are any bear warnings or trail closures due to bear problems.

Allow plenty of time for your trip. Often people think that they can accomplish many goals in the mountains in a day or two and return, not realizing that the steepness of the terrain, the elevation, and sudden changes in weather can all cause the trip to take much longer than expected.

Remember to set your limit and to know when to turn back when any member of the group cannot safely continue. The mountain will still be there for another day.

The majority of people I have guided on high mountain outings have not been in shape for the rigors of the trip. Also, you must be acclimated to the higher elevation. Coming from a city located near sea level and trying to climb a mountain that is over 10,000 feet high within a day or two is almost impossible and downright dangerous. In addition, fatigue causes bad judgment and carelessness, both of which have killed many people in the mountains.

In planning your trip, be sure that you have the proper equipment for the terrain and for the weather conditions that you can expect. Early in my career, I learned a hard lesson about wearing the right equipment in the Rocky Mountains. For quite some time I resisted buying a cowboy hat. I didn't want to look like a character from a Zane Grey novel on the high mountain trails. The local guides I was working with kept telling me that the day would come when I would wish I had a cowboy hat. I realized just how right they were one afternoon when a violent hailstorm hit our packstring. There was nowhere to go, and my head, face, and neck took a tremendous beating as golf ball-sized hail pounded us for fifteen minutes. Needless to say, as soon as I arrived back in civilization, I bought a cowboy hat.

Choose all mountain equipment carefully. If you doubt your ability to select the right equipment, get advice from someone who knows the area you are going into and who is an outfitter.

DESERTS

Travel in hot, dry deserts can be an enjoyable outing to those who are adequately prepared and knowledgeable as to its possible hazards. To the unprepared, though, it can be a horrible experience.

Walking

When in the desert, even travelers in good physical condition should walk slowly and rest about ten minutes per hour. At this rate, a person in good physical condition can initially cover about ten to twelve miles per day. After he becomes fatigued or if he lacks sufficient water or food, this distance becomes less.

Walking at night may be a good idea, because it is cooler then, and if lack of water is a problem, you will dehydrate less. However, the disadvantages are that you may not be able to see the ground well enough and may stumble or overlook water or food sources or signs of habitation. Another factor to consider in the desert is that rattlesnakes are active at night, so you may get too close to one without even realizing it, until you hear the telltale rattle. It is usually best to travel in the desert in early morning or late evening, spending midday in whatever shade may be available. Also, the position of the sun early and late in the day will give you a better sense of direction.

Pick the easiest and safest way to walk. Go around obstacles instead of over them. Rather than going up or down steep slopes, zigzag to prevent undue exertion. Go around gullies and canyons instead of through them. Watch for snakes, especially at night, because the desert is home to many rattlesnakes. When walking in sand, lean well forward, keeping your knees bent. When walking with companions, adjust the rate to the slowest person.

During breaks, try to sit down in the shade and prop your feet up high, remove your shoes and change socks, or straighten the ones you are wearing. If the ground is too hot to sit on, no shade is available, and you cannot raise your feet, do not remove your shoes, because you may not be able to get them back onto swollen feet. However, you can unlace boots or shoes, adjust socks, and re-lace.

Since shade may not be easy to find in a desert environment, the desert survival kit should contain a metallic plastic sheet, such as the MCR Medical Emergency Blanket. This silver sheet folds up to the size of a deck of playing cards and can be unfolded into a quick shade shelter by attaching it to rocks or brush with cord. Due to its silver color, it also serves as a signal, and at night, when the temperature drops, you can wrap up in it to stay warm.

Driving

Driving can be hazardous on little-used desert roads, but if a few simple suggestions are followed, desert driving can be done safely. Have a map of the area you are going into. Obtain current information from the highway patrol, conservation officer, or county sheriff's office as to the conditions of the roads in that area. Have a vehicle that is in good condition that is designed for off-road travel. Drive slowly. If in doubt about the terrain, stop and check it out first on foot. Do not attempt to drive on questionable roads without first checking the footing and clearances. High centers on rocks may rupture the oil pan. Washes may cause the powered wheels to become suspended above the ground.

In sand, the wheels may sink, resulting in a high center and loss of traction. Avoid spinning wheels to gain motion, because this will only cause the wheels to dig in further. Instead, apply power very slowly. Consider reducing tire pressure before you get in too deep.

Under emergency conditions, when driving in sand, traction can be increased by partially deflating tires. Be careful not to remove so much air that the tire may slip on the rim. Then, drive slowly. Start, stop, and turn gradually because sudden motions cause wheels to dig in.

Be sure to take these tools and equipment if you intend to drive off the main roads: one or more shovels, a pick, a tow chain or cable, at least fifty feet of strong nylon tow rope, portable air compressor, ax, full water containers, at least two full gas cans, extra fan belts, and your regular spare parts and auto tools. Include a survival kit and a tarp or means of creating a large area of shade. Be sure that your fuel tank is full, and that you have a filled, clean radiator, a filled battery, and new fan belts. If you become stuck or your car breaks down, raise the hood and stay with the car. The raised hood is an indication to other desert travelers that you need help.

Your vehicle can provide you with life-saving shade. In fact, one of the best shelters you can utilize if you are stranded is your vehicle. First of all, don't get into the vehicle because it will be like an oven. What you want is a double layer of insulation between the sun and you, and your car or truck can provide this. Here's how to construct a shelter:

1. Open all of the vehicle doors and windows for ventilation. Disconnect interior car lights that come on when doors are open. This will conserve the battery for other uses.
2. Using a shovel, board, or hubcap, scoop the dirt out from under the vehicle, away from the motor, tailpipe, or muffler, as they will all be hot. Dig away the top fifteen inches or more, the deeper the cooler.
3. Be sure to dig under the side or end of the vehicle where the shade is.
4. Take your time and avoid getting too hot.
5. Once you have the trench dug, crawl in and enjoy the shade. The ground temperature down fifteen inches deep should not be more than the mid-80s.
6. Be sure you have your ground-to-air signals out, and stay alert for rescue aircraft. If you decide to work on your vehicle or enlarge your shelter, wait until the cool of the evening.

Since the roof of the vehicle takes much of the sun's heat and the floor of the vehicle takes the secondary heat, the space under the vehicle can be one of the best shelters in the desert. Stay with your vehicle. Desert search and rescue experts state that many desert deaths occur within two hours after the victim leaves his shelter.

Dress for the Environment

In the desert, you should wear light-colored clothing to reflect some of the heat of the sun. Be sure to keep your clothing on, as clothing helps ration your sweat by slowing the evaporation rate and prolonging the cooling effect. It also helps keep out the hot desert air. Long-sleeve shirts and broad-brimmed hats are also recommended

Remember that deserts can be cold during the night, so a jacket in your daypack could be a welcome item of clothing if an unplanned night in the desert occurs.

It is much cooler to seek shade in a hot desert by digging down under the rear of a vehicle than to stay inside. The vehicle becomes an oven quickly.

Basic Rules for Desert Survival

By following a few basic rules, you can assure yourself of a safer trip into the desert:

1. Never go into the desert without filing a trip plan with responsible adults. Stick to the plan.
2. Carry at least one gallon of water per person per day.

3. Watch the weather. Even though a desert is a dry environment, flash floods can occur rapidly even if the rain may not fall where you are. Avoid travel in low areas if thunderstorms are on the horizon.
4. Carry a survival kit and a means of constructing quick shade.
5. Stay hydrated.
6. If water is limited, keep your mouth shut and breathe through your nose. Keep talking to a minimum, do not eat, and do not take salt.
7. Do not sit or lie directly on the ground, which may be 30 F degrees hotter than the air. Sit on your daypack.
8. A roadway is a sign of civilization. If you find a road, stay on it, for there's a good chance that help will happen along.
9. Always carry a charged cell phone.
10. If you become lost or stranded, stay put in the shade and put out signals.

RIVERS, LAKES, OCEAN

The ability to survive on streams and large bodies of water varies greatly, from a kayak trip on a creek to an offshore fishing trip on a large boat. The one thing they all have in common is in the planning.

Open bodies of water, be they rivers, lakes, or oceans, are subject to become dangerous quickly due to changes in the weather, such as thunderstorms bringing lightning, wind, and heavy rain, all which can make travel dangerous. Because of this, always check out the weather forecasts for the dates of your float trip or offshore excursion. During the trip, a sharp eye should always be kept on the weather.

Wear and carry clothing that is appropriate for the weather and wet conditions you may encounter. Hypothermia is a real threat for trips on water. In Nunavut Territory Canada not long ago, I got severe hypothermia just from the spray of a motorboat on a huge lake.

Regardless of whether a float trip is a half-day trip down a local river or an overnight deep-sea fishing excursion, a trip plan needs to be filed with responsible people.

For canoe, kayak, raft, and rowboat trips that require paddling or rowing, every member of the group should be in decent physical condition for the trip. These types of trips demand that you use muscles that you probably don't use otherwise, or at least don't use often. Beyond hours of non-stop paddling, there could be lifting the watercraft, portaging, or lifting or pulling the watercraft over logs or down shallow rapids. Be in shape for the trip. To not be could result in a stranding and the need for rescue.

Anytime you are on water in any type watercraft, having and using an approved personal flotation device (PFD) is a must and a legal requirement.

For float trips on creeks, rivers, and lakes, having extra paddles can be a lifesaver. If a motor is used, then spare parts and a tool kit are a must, as is a fire extinguisher. All water craft should have a repair kit suitable for that craft onboard and a member of the group who has the mechanical skills to make repairs. I was on a several-weeks-long remote canoe trip in northern Canada when a roll of duct tape allowed me to repair a hole in my canoe and the trip continued; otherwise I would have been stranded.

Swim or float downstream feet first.

A canoe, raft, or boat overturn in rapids requires quick thinking to protect the head from being banged on rocks. Always float feet first to give the head protection, plus this allows the survivor to see where he needs to go.

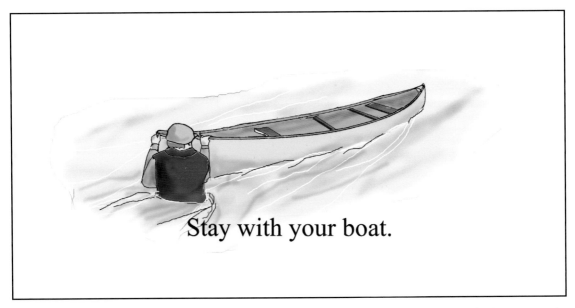

Stay with your boat.

In a boat, canoe, or raft overturn on a large lake or ocean, if the watercraft doesn't sink, stay with the floating platform as it is much easier for rescue spotters to see the watercraft than a person floating in a large body of water.

If you plan to take a trip out into a large body of water such as an ocean, bay, or sprawling inland lake, make sure that the boat you take is of a size and design to match the conditions that may be met on the trip. Boats of this size should have modern navigational aids, two-way radios capable of talking to the Coast Guard, and a seasoned boat pilot. Large open water can become dangerous in just minutes from sudden weather changes, an equipment failure, or accident such as a fire on board. Use caution when planning a trip of this type and get the best boat and crew for the conditions. Study ocean survival before you take such a trip. If the water is cold where you plan your ocean trip, be sure the boat is equipped with survival suits and that you know how to get into one and use it correctly. In cold water, they are a must.

If your float trip involves a boat with a motor, make sure you take enough fuel. The Coast Guard will tell you that many boaters get into trouble both on ocean trips and in large backcountry lakes simply because they run out of fuel. Be sure the tanks of the boat you are in are full before leaving the dock. Don't take a trip so long that you can't reach your destination on a third of a tank. Plan on a third going out, a third returning, and a third in reserve for emergencies.

Trips on small streams and lakes should start with each person having a personal flotation device (PFD) and knowing how to float in it to slow hypothermia. Most survival situations in this environment start with a capsized watercraft and everyone in the water. If rapids are part of the trip, then they need to know that if the craft has been overturned or sunk, they need to go down rapids feet-first with their legs acting as shock absorbers as they hit rocks.

On large lakes where the shore may be too far away to swim to, assuming the watercraft doesn't sink, stay with the craft as it is much easier for searchers to spot you hanging onto the craft by searchers and it doesn't take as much energy if you hang onto the side of the craft.

Also each person on the trip needs to have a survival kit attached to them because as soon as they make the shore the basics of wilderness survival kick in. Be sure to set up your survival camp near the shore as that will be the first place search and rescue will be looking.

Finally, do not forget that the one of the most common causes of small watercraft accidents is overloading. Never take on more passengers than the watercraft is designed to hold.

SWAMPS

The word "swamp" means many things to many people. To some, it is a forbidding, wet environment that humans should avoid at all costs. To others, it is an adventurous place rich in scenery, nature, game, and fish, a locale where peace of mind comes easy.

Webster's Dictionary defines swamp as "wet spongy land saturated and sometimes partially or intermittently covered with water." The US Department of the Interior's Fish and Wildlife Service has an official definition: "Swamp is all wetlands with greater than 50 percent of its area in cover of woody plants; that is, trees, brush, vines, etc."

Many people confuse marshlands with swamps. Marshes are almost totally devoid of any bushes or trees. Most marshes are created by tidal activity, and they are usually in areas with high saline or alkaline content in the soil. Marshes are usually covered in grass-like plants and are usually associated with the ocean.

Other people mistake bogs for swamps. Bogs are usually the remains of ancient lakes. While swamps have a covering of trees and woody plants, bogs are covered with mosses, ferns, and

A typical peat bog.

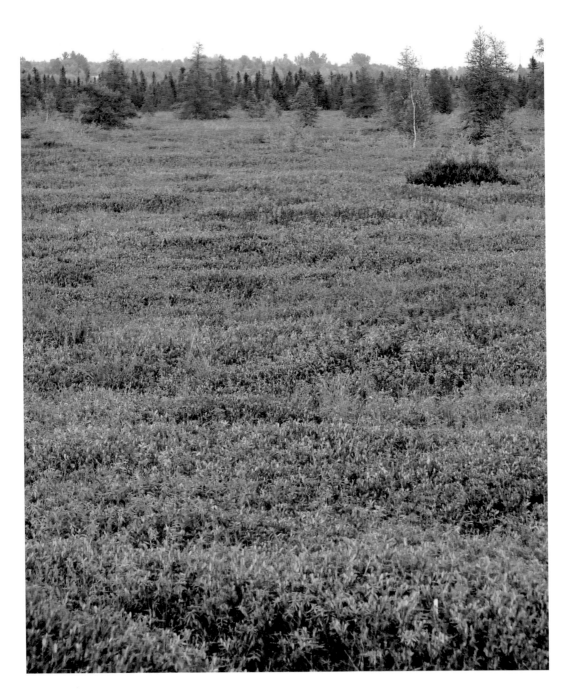

lichens. Until you step in a bog, you usually don't see the water. Then the bog acts like a wet sponge.

There are swamps in almost every region of North America. This comes as a surprise to many people who normally think of swamps as something found only in the Deep South.

The origins of swamps are varied. Many are the result of centuries of change in river flows. Swamps along the Mississippi River and the Ohio River were formed this way. Some swamps are the result of glacial activities—swamps in Canada, around the Great Lakes, and in New England are of this type. Still other swamps were created by falling meteorites, such as the Carolina Bays; by receding ocean, such as the Okefenokee Swamp; or by an earthquake, such as Reelfoot Swamp. Today new swamps are being created at a rapid rate by the activity of beavers. There seem to be almost as many ways that swamps are created as there, are swamps.

When you begin to consider exploring, hunting, fishing, camping, canoeing, or trapping in the swamps, you may be surprised at how much negative feedback you will hear about swamps in general. For centuries, Americans have been kept out of nature-rich swamps by horror tales and negative folklore. Quicksand . . . black panthers . . . snakes . . . spiders . . . alligators . . . lost! These associations and others have been too often connected with swamps. Television and movies have capitalized on these fears in misleading movies filmed in so-called swamp settings.

Historians tell us that this fear of swamps came about during the early exploration of North America. Since there are few swamps in Europe, the European explorers avoided swamps. Lack of experience with this new swamp environment made them mysterious to explorers. Native Americans were quick to recognize white men's fear of swamps and told them frightening stories to keep the swamps to themselves. With the passing of each generation these swamp stories grew and were handed down as fact. We still have many swamp phobias with us today that are the result of centuries-old tales.

Swamps are among our last wilderness areas, and many of them offer a backcountry setting near urban areas. Because of the fear and ignorance so many people have of swamps, there are still many swamps scattered over North America that remain totally wild. These swamps serve many beneficial purposes and we are fortunate that we have them. They are the last preserves for many of our endangered plants and animals. They are also great water storage areas and are constantly recharging underground water supplies. The trees and lush plants in swamps help keep us in oxygen.

Of equal importance is the swamp's role in providing recreation and adventure. Swamps are excellent fauna and flora habitats; nowhere will you find better hunting and fishing. Because swamps are rich in suitable wildlife habitat and have suffered less from the pressures of progress than any other parts of the American landscape, they constitute the outdoorsman's last paradise. At the same time, swamps may suddenly require survival skills.

Why Are Swamps Difficult?

Because a swamp is a wet environment in which there are few roads and thick vegetation, it can put you in a survival predicament quickly. Basically, there are three common swamp predicaments that are dangerous.

1. With the debris typical in swamp water, it is easy to foul an outboard motor or to puncture a canoe, kayak, inflatable raft; or for a four-wheel-drive vehicle to become hopelessly stuck in the always unpredictable mud and muck.
2. It is easy to get lost. Since swamp terrain is generally flat, everything tends to look alike on an overcast day. Much of the vegetation in the swamp looks the same, and landmarks are often near impossible to establish or recognize.
3. You or a group member could become sick or injured and not be able to get help. Strandings in swamps are often difficult to avoid. A top priority when you go into a swamp should always be to let someone know where you are going and when you plan to return. File a trip plan. Always keep your equipment in good repair and have a back-up system or at least a repair kit that you know how to use. Avoid weather that could get you into trouble, and avoid areas from which your return may be impossible In other words, anytime you are venturing into a swamp, use common sense.

No one should ever go into a swamp alone. Be sure to let your group know generally where you plan to explore, hunt, fish, or hike, and when you plan to return. Also tell someone at your home, motel, or lodge where you are going and when you plan to return.

An extra precaution is to leave a note on the windshield of your car stating your name, the direction in which you are traveling, and when you plan to return. While these basic rules, which I emphasize many times in this book, can't prevent you from having an immobilizing accident, they can cut down on the number of hours your ordeal lasts.

Swamps are also difficult because they are watery environments, and travel in a straight line is usually impossible for any great distance. Following the known water course across the swamp often defies most navigational principles. In most cases, a local guide who is familiar with the swamp is a must if you are to go from one point to another in a reasonable amount of time.

Swamp Survival Techniques

Techniques for surviving in a swamp are very similar to techniques discussed throughout this book. However, there are a few points peculiar to swamp survival that should be emphasized.

Making it easier to be found.

Once you realize that you are lost in a swamp, the very first thing you need to do is to stop. A swamp is no place to be wandering about. The same thing applies if you are stranded, as by a hole in your kayak or canoe, or an outboard motor which has stopped. Don't attempt to walk out. Stay where you are, or move only a short distance to get into a more open area where you may be spotted easily from the air.

The importance of an opening cannot be overemphasized in the case of a swamp. Many times I have been looking in a swamp for someone who was lost and had a canoe or boat with him. Because of the lush overhead vegetation, I have flown over such people without ever seeing them.

If you have a boat or canoe, try to secure it where it can be seen from overhead. Once you have an opening in which to await rescue, use some sort of signal so that you will be more easily

A marsh.

spotted. Review Chapter 10 in this book on signaling. Also use your imagination. However, many times in the case of a boat or canoe, once it is in the opening, it is easily spotted from the air, especially if those who are searching for you know that you were traveling by boat or canoe.

Protection from the elements.

Once you have established an opening in which to await rescue, the first thing to consider is what protections are necessary. During cool or cold weather in a swamp, hypothermia is one of the first concerns, being in a wet environment, being tired, being scared, all go together to bring on hypothermia. As quickly as possible, build a fire. Even in this wet environment, a fire can be started by following the techniques discussed in Chapter 9.

Obviously, if you have to await rescue in a boat because getting on dry land is impossible or not practical, bundle up as much as you can to prevent hypothermia. Consider putting on raingear to cut the chilling effect of the wind.

If you are caught in a swamp during warm weather, your immediate attention may be directed to protection from mosquitoes and blackflies. These biting insects are just as dangerous as, if not more dangerous than, any snakes or other critters you are likely to run into in the swamps. Take plenty of insect repellent with you and long sleeve shirt and long pants.

Lightning is another danger during warm weather. As an example of how terrifying lightning can be, several years ago I was guiding an Ohio fisherman in a swamp in East Texas when a sudden and fierce thunderstorm hit. We were caught out in some tall timber. I asked my client to lie down in the boat and prepared to crank the motor and move into a stand of thick, low-growing brush. He was shocked that I would even think of putting the boat into that "cottonmouth-infested brush." As he was preaching to me the dangers of snakes, a bolt of lightning clobbered a nearby cypress with an earsplitting crack. Pieces of bark flew in all directions. My client dived into the bottom of the boat and begged me to get into the low-growing bushes. The storm lasted two long hours, with the severity of a mortar attack. On the way back to camp, my pale client told me that snakes were now only his second-biggest fear in the swamp—lightning was first!

Drinking water.

You'd think that the last problem you'd have in a swamp survival situation would be that of finding water. Granted, there is usually plenty of water available in most swamps, but many times the water is not safe to drink. In fact, most swamps offer few, if any, sources of safe drinking water. Many of today's swamps are fed by waters that originate upstream, and these streams may be polluted by waste from cities, industries, agricultural areas, and even rural septic tanks. Regardless of how clear the swamp water may look, don't trust it. Some swamps that are made up primarily of standing water contain stagnant water that is subject to bacteriological contamination from animals. Other swamps, such as the rapidly growing number of beaver swamps, contain populations of animals that carry a variety of potential illnesses to man.

The National Park Service states, "We know of no swamp waters that have met a safe drinking water test." It is only good judgment to purify the water regardless of how pure it may look. I can testify that this is true. Several years ago two of my friends went deep into a swamp in southern Mississippi on a week-long search for bull bluegills. The running water next to their camp looked

A typical swamp of the Deep South.

so clean that they didn't bother to treat it. That was a mistake that cut their trip short. They were weeks getting their digestive systems back into proper working order.

Needless to say, if you're dying of thirst, the long-range effect of drinking contaminated water is something you will have to worry about later. However, if it is at all possible to treat the water you are going to drink, you should do so. Chapter 11 in this book concerning drinking water is very important. With the modern methods of treating water, there is no excuse for not having good water to drink while you are in the swamp, even in a survival situation. Think ahead. If your swamp trip takes you far from treated water, go prepared. Take enough water with you and take along a method of treating the water.

Gear for swamp survival is very similar to survival gear for other areas. Many times in southern swamps, I have used the same survival kit that I use in the Arctic. However, also be sure to have insect repellent, a good supply of waterproof matches, and, if possible, a machete. The machete is one of the best survival knives in a swamp environment. It can do much to make your stay more comfortable. It can be used for everything from simple camp chores to opening up a clearing where you can be seen from' overhead.

The person who finds him- or herself stranded or lost in a swamp has little to fear, provided he has filed a trip plan and carries a survival kit with him. Many of the fears associated with swamps are unfounded.

15

WHEN A MEMBER OF YOUR GROUP IS MISSING

Have you been on an outing when you suddenly realized you were lost or stranded, unable to return to camp or your vehicle? If not, get ready, because if you go into the backcountry enough, chances are it will happen eventually. As a wildlife professional, I have spent considerable time looking for missing people in the outdoors. Most of the time, they are simply turned around in the woods and are easily found.

However, some are injured and unable to move, often due to a fall. Once, a guide who worked for me fell into an abandoned well.

Unfortunately, some outdoor enthusiasts are brought out dead as a result of heart attacks, falls, or hypothermia. The cause of death is often brought on by the stress of being lost.

While many outdoor people are learning what to do if they should become lost or stranded, few know what to do if their buddy does not make it back to the car or camp when he or she is supposed to. Every group, be it an outing club or just two friends, should plan ahead for that moment when one of them is missing. This is just as important if you are exploring on your own back forty as in a remote wilderness.

It should be a policy that every member of the group let the others know specifically where he is going and when he plans to return. All members of the group should agree to sit tight once they realize they are lost. This should be stressed over and over again. Every member of the group should carry a compass (that they know how to use), a GPS, a map of the area, cell phone, a knife, and a survival kit.

Know the medical condition of your companions. If a member of your group has a heart problem, seizures, or other medical problem, make sure a buddy goes with him. An unconscious person needs to be found quickly, but is extremely difficult to find.

Each member of your group needs to know how to locate the nearest conservation officer, forest ranger, or sheriff's office. In most counties in the US, the local sheriff is responsible for search and rescue. Everyone should carry the phone numbers of these officials. Delay in getting trained search-and-rescue help can be deadly.

Always be aware of how your fellow companions are dressed, what type boots they wear, and the state of mind they are in. This information is extremely valuable to search officials.

The most crucial time during a missing-buddy crisis is when you first realize that he or she is late coming into camp or back on the trail and you get no answers to your signals. Don't panic. The first rule is to stay calm and think. In most cases, lost or stranded situations are merely a sobering two- or three-hour adventure.

Signaling is an important part of the early search, as rescued people often state that while they were lost or stranded, they thought no one would bother to look for them. Select a logical point, such as where he or she was last seen, the logging road or field nearest the "most likely" area, camp, or vehicle, and blow an automobile horn or whistle. Either of these signals is an indication to the missing person that someone is looking for him. If he is nearby, he can walk to the sound. For this reason, it is crucial to blow the horn or whistle in bursts of three so that it is obviously a signal and not some unrelated noise. Pause between bursts of three and listen carefully for a reply. If the missing person has a whistle, and he should, you may hear a response immediately. If you are getting no response to your initial signaling, and feel that your buddy may be in trouble, seek out a forest ranger, conservation officer, or sheriff's department official to get trained search-and-rescue people on the scene as soon as possible. If you leave to obtain professional help, leave someone at the signal point; while one person goes for help, another should stay to continue signaling and listening.

Attempting to set up your own search is generally a bad idea, since most often untrained people with the best of intentions usually do more harm than good. They destroy valuable clues and often become lost or hurt themselves. Searching for missing people is a skill best left to those trained.

However, in some specific circumstances, such as when help is hours away or when the tract of land is not large and it is known almost exactly where the missing person is likely to be, fellow outdoorsmen might conduct a limited search. In those exceptional cases, follow these guidelines:

1. Get the entire group together to plan your search.
2. To help identify clues that you find, find out what each member knows, such as when and where the missing person was last seen, what their trip plan was, what brand of candy they eat, what type of sole do they have on their boots and their size, where they most likely went, and so on.
3. Establish someone in the group as leader of the search, and everyone does as he or she says.
4. Leave someone at the original spot to continue signaling.
5. If a specific spot is known, two searchers should begin the search with thorough examination of that immediate area in case there was a health problem or injury. Take care not to destroy any signs. It is important that only one or two do this, as a larger group will destroy clues that might be helpful if a professional search is needed.
6. Look for signs, such as tracks, for an indication of the missing person's direction of travel.
7. Due to the excitement of the moment, searchers often get lost themselves, so mark the trail you take in so you can follow it out.

8. Consider what sounds the missing person can hear—farm, railroad, highway, mill whistle, etc.—and send someone to that location. Rather than sit still, many lost people will try to walk to sounds such as these.

9. If there are roads around the area, a vehicle should patrol these roads regularly, but do not blow the horn as you travel as the lost person will start in the direction of the horn, only to have it change directions. I have found lost people who would have been found quickly if they hadn't spent the night chasing the sounds of moving truck horns.

10. If there is a long opening in the area, such as railroad tracks, gas line, electric line right-of-way, or large fields, have someone watch these areas with binoculars.

11. Plan a signal or specific time for calling off the search. If the missing person has not been found within a short time, turn the search over to professionals.

If you and your outdoor companions have prepared for the day one of you is missing, chances are you will never be faced with a tragedy.

APPENDIX I

BSA REQUIREMENTS FOR THE WILDERNESS SURVIVAL MERIT BADGE:

1. Do the following:

   (a) Explain to your counselor the hazards you are most likely to encounter while participating in wilderness survival activities, and what you should do to anticipate, help prevent, mitigate, or lessen these hazards.

   (b) Show that you know first aid for and how to prevent injuries or illnesses likely to occur in backcountry settings, including hypothermia, heat reactions, frostbite, dehydration, blisters, insect stings, tick bites, and snakebites.

2. From memory list the seven priorities for survival in a backcountry or wilderness location. Explain the importance of each one with your counselor.

3. Describe ways to avoid panic and maintain a high level of morale when lost, and explain why this is important.

4. Describe the steps you would take to survive in the following exposure conditions:

   (a) Cold and snowy

   (b) Wet

   (c) Hot and dry

   (d) Windy

   (e) At or on the water

5. Put together a personal survival kit and be able to explain how each item in it could be useful.

6. Using three different methods (other than matches), build and light three fires.

7. Do the following:

   (a) Show five different ways to attract attention when lost.

   (b) Demonstrate how to use a signal mirror.

   (c) Describe from memory five ground-to-air signals and tell what they mean.

8. Improvise a natural shelter. For the purpose of this demonstration, use techniques that have little negative impact on the environment. Spend a night in your shelter.
9. Explain how to protect yourself from insects, reptiles, bears, and other animals of the local region.
10. Demonstrate three ways to treat water found in the outdoors to prepare it for drinking.
11. Show that you know the proper clothing to wear while in the outdoors during extremely hot and cold weather and during wet conditions.
12. Explain why it usually is not wise to eat edible wild plants or wildlife in a wilderness survival situation.

APPENDIX II

WEB ADDRESSES FOR SURVIVAL PRODUCTS MENTIONED IN THIS BOOK

Adventure Medical Kits – www.adventuremedicalkits.com
After Bite/After Burn – www.afterbite.com
BugX Insect Repellent – www.coretexproducts.com
Coghlan's Tube Tent – www.coghlans.com
FireSteel Magnesium Rod – www.firesteel.com
Fox 40 Whistle – www.fox40world.com
LifeStraw Water Filter – www.lifestraw.com
MRC Medical Emergency Sleeping Bag – www.mrcmedical.com
Potable Aqua Water Treatment Tablets – www.potableaqua.com
Sawyer Water Filter – www.sawyer.com
Spot Personal Locator Beacon – www.findmespot.com
StarFlash Signal Mirror – www.ultimatesurvival.com
SureFire Flashlights – www.surefire.com
ThermaCell Insect Repellent – www.thermacell.com
WindStorm Whistle – www.stormwhistles.com